Practical Machine Learning and Image Processing

For Facial Recognition, Object Detection, and Pattern Recognition Using Python

Himanshu Singh

Apress®

Practical Machine Learning and Image Processing

Himanshu Singh
Allahabad, Uttar Pradesh, India

ISBN-13 (pbk): 978-1-4842-4148-6 ISBN-13 (electronic): 978-1-4842-4149-3
https://doi.org/10.1007/978-1-4842-4149-3

Library of Congress Control Number: 2019933848

Managing Director, Apress Media LLC: Welmoed Spahr
Acquisitions Editor: Celestin Suresh John
Development Editor: Matthew Moodie
Coordinating Editor: Aditee Mirashi

Cover designed by eStudioCalamar
Cover image designed by Freepik (www.freepik.com)

Distributed to the book trade worldwide by Springer Science+Business Media New York, 233 Spring Street, 6th Floor, New York, NY 10013. Phone 1-800-SPRINGER, fax (201) 348-4505, e-mail orders-ny@springer-sbm.com, or visit www.springeronline.com. Apress Media, LLC is a California LLC and the sole member (owner) is Springer Science + Business Media Finance Inc (SSBM Finance Inc). SSBM Finance Inc is a **Delaware** corporation.

For information on translations, please e-mail rights@apress.com, or visit http://www.apress.com/rights-permissions.

Apress titles may be purchased in bulk for academic, corporate, or promotional use. eBook versions and licenses are also available for most titles. For more information, reference our Print and eBook Bulk Sales web page at http://www.apress.com/bulk-sales.

Any source code or other supplementary material referenced by the author in this book is available to readers on GitHub via the book's product page, located at www.apress.com/978-1-4842-4148-6. For more detailed information, please visit http://www.apress.com/source-code.

Printed on acid-free paper

Table of Contents

About the Author

Himanshu Singh has more than 6+ years of experience as a data science professional. Currently, he is a senior data scientist at V-Soft Labs. He provides corporate training on data science, machine learning, and deep learning. He is also a visiting faculty member in analytics at the Narsee Monjee Institute of Management Studies, considered one of the premium management institutes in India. He is founder of Black Feathers Analytics and Rise of Literati Clubs.

About the Technical Reviewer

Santanu Pattanayak currently works at GE, Digital, as a staff data scientist and is author of *Pro Deep Learning with TensorFlow: A Mathematical Approach to Advanced Artificial Intelligence in Python*. He has approximately 12 years of overall work experience, with eight of years of experience in the data analytics/data science field, and also has a background in development and database technologies. Before joining GE, Santanu worked in companies such as RBS, Capgemini, and IBM. He graduated with a degree in electrical engineering from Jadavpur University, Kolkata, and is an avid math enthusiast. Santanu is currently pursuing a master's degree in data science from the Indian Institute of Technology, Hyderabad. He also devotes his time to data science hackathons and Kaggle competitions in which he ranks within the top 500 worldwide. Santanu was born and brought up in West Bengal, India, and currently resides in Bangalore, India, with his wife.

Acknowledgments

First of all, I thank the Apress Team, Celestian John and Aditee Mirashi, for giving me a platform to contribute my image processing knowledge and share it with readers. Second, I thank my colleagues, without whom this book would not have been possible: Aravind Kota, Yamuna, and my boss and mentor, Yunis Ahmad Lone. I also thank my students. They helped me see which issues are challenging for them, and enabled me to devise a specific means of explaining the concepts to them in a manner that facilitates their learning.

Last, but not the least, I thank my wife, Shikha Singh. Her constant support and help has allowed this project to come to fruition. She assisted me in all aspects of writing this book, sometimes proofreading and writing technical details herself.

Many thanks to everyone for your constant support.

Introduction

Practical Machine Learning and Image Processing gives readers deep insight into the basics of image processing and various image processing methodologies and algorithms, applications using various Python libraries, and real-time use case implementation using machine learning approaches.

The book begins with a discussion of the setup environment for different operating systems, presents basic image processing terminology, and explores useful Python concepts for algorithm application. It then delves into various image processing algorithms and practical implementation of them in Python using two libraries: Scikit Image and OpenCV. Next, advanced machine learning and deep learning methods are presented for image processing and classification. Concepts such as Adaboost, XG Boost, convolutional neural networks, and more, for image-specific applications are explained. Later, the process for making models in real time and then deploying them is described.

All the concepts in the book are explained using real-life scenarios. By the end of the book, readers should be able to apply image processing techniques and make machine learning models for customized applications.

CHAPTER 1

Setup Environment

In this chapter we prepare our system to run the code included in this book. Let's look at how to install the following:

- Anaconda
- OpenCV
- Keras

Aside from the last two packages in the list, most of what we need comes preinstalled with Anaconda. Let's start with Anaconda, then follow with OpenCV and Keras.

Install Anaconda

The Anaconda installation page proclaims it is "The Most Popular Python Data Science Platform." Using Anaconda, installing supporting software, setting up virtual environments, and so on, are all quite easy, and the package comes with one of the best integrated development environments (IDEs) for Python data science: Jupyter Notebook. Jupyter not only helps you write Python code, but also it makes your code look beautiful and presentable. So, let's get started with the Anaconda installation.

H. Singh, *Practical Machine Learning and Image Processing*,
https://doi.org/10.1007/978-1-4842-4149-3_1

Windows

If you are using Windows, here's the process:

1. Go to `www.anaconda.com`.
2. On the top right side of the screen , is the button Downloads. Click it.
3. Scroll down and you will see two versions of Anaconda: Python version 3.7 and Python version 2.7. In the Python 3.7 version box, select 64-Bit Graphical Installer (select the 32-bit option, if your system is a 32-bit system).
4. Wait for the download to finish, then double-click the installation file.
5. Finish the installation and restart your system.
6. Now, open the Start menu, search for the Anaconda prompt, and select it. A shell named Anaconda Prompt appears. Type `Jupyter Notebook` inside the shell and you will see a screen like the one displayed in Figure 1-1.

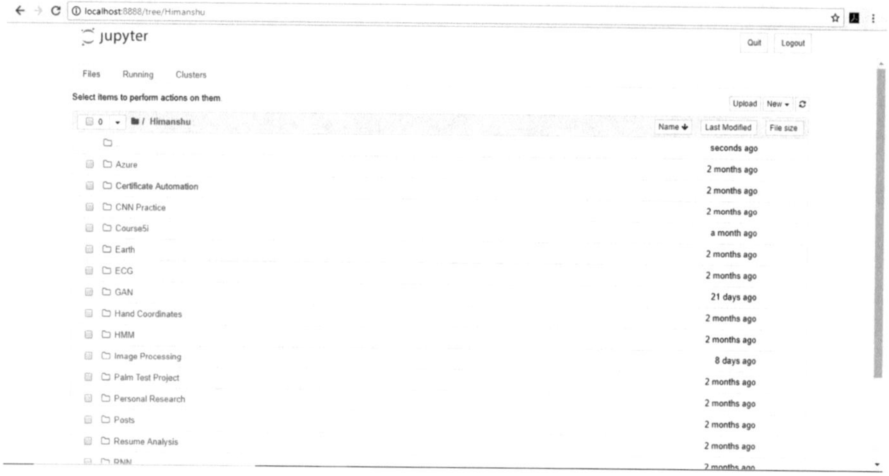

Figure 1-1. *Opening screen*

7. In the top right corner of the Files tab, you'll see the drop-down New. Click the downward-pointing arrow and Select Python 3. Now you're ready to code (Figure 1-2)!

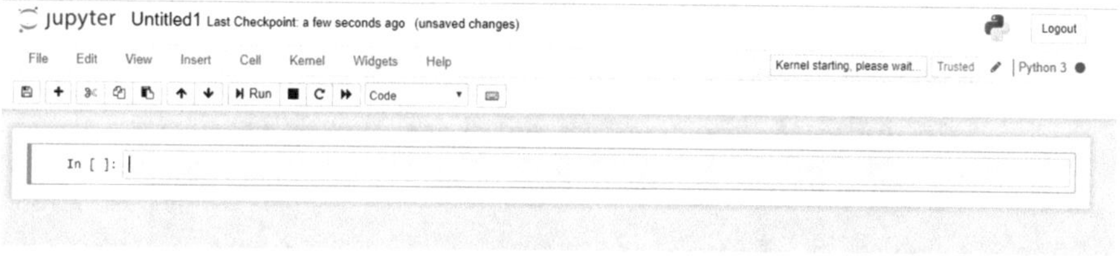

Figure 1-2. *A new Python script*

macOS

If you are using macOS, here is the Anaconda installation process:

1. Download Anaconda for macOS as you would for Windows.
2. Double-click the .pkg file and follow the installation procedures.
3. Open your terminal and type `Jupyter Notebook`. You will see the same screen shown in Figure 1-1.

Ubuntu

The process for downloading Anaconda in Ubuntu is as follows:

1. Download Anaconda for Linux as you did for Windows.
2. Go to the installation folder and type `bash Anaconda-latest-Linux-x86_64.sh`.
3. Follow the installation procedures, open your terminal, and type `Jupyter Notebook`. You will see the same screen shown in Figure 1-1.

Install OpenCV

Now that we have installed Anaconda and Jupyter Notebook. The next thing to do is to install its supporting software. For OpenCV, do the following:

1. Open the Anaconda Prompt.
2. Type `conda install -c conda-forge opencv`.

3. You could also type `conda install -c conda-forge/label/broken opencv`.

4. After a few minutes, OpenCV will be installed in your environment.

Install Keras

To install Keras, follow these procedures:

1. Open the Anaconda Prompt.

Type `conda install -c conda-forge keras.`

2. After a few minutes, Keras will be installed in your environment.

Test the Installations

Before going further, you need to test the installations as follows:

1. Open Jupyter Notebook.

2. Open a new Python 3 notebook.

3. Type `import cv2`. If you do not receive an error, then OpenCV has been installed perfectly. If an error comes, either you did something wrong during the installation, or there may be a compatibility issue. For rectification, either restart the process of installation, or refer to OpenCV documentation page.

4. Type `import keras`. If you do not receive an error, then Keras has been installed perfectly. If an error comes, either you did something wrong during the installation, or there may be a compatibility issue. For rectification, either restart the process of installation, or refer to Keras documentation page.

Virtual Environments

Now that we have installed the software we need, let's take a look at virtual environments. Virtual environments are very important when you want to develop multiple projects. What should we do if we are developing a product using Python 3, but we want to create another project using Python 2.7? If we do it directly, we may encounter problems because different versions of Python are installed. Or, we could create a virtual environment, install Python 2.7, and develop the product inside that environment. Regardless of what you develop inside a virtual environment, it never influences any code outside the environment. Let's see how we can create a virtual environment:

1. Type `conda create -n environment_name python=version anaconda`. In place of `environment_name`, type any name you wish to give to your environment. In place of `version`, type any version of Python that you wish to use (for example, 2.7, 3.5, 3.6, and so on).
2. Now that we have created the environment, we have to activate it. We do this by typing `source activate environment_name`.
3. We can now open Jupyter Notebook and start working in this environment.
4. To deactivate the environment, type `source deactivate`.

CHAPTER 2

Introduction to Image Processing

In this chapter we examine exactly what an image is, and its related properties. By the end of the chapter, you should have an understanding of the following concepts:

- Images
- Pixels
- Image resolution
- Pixels per inch (PPI) and dots per inch (DPI)
- Bitmap images
- Lossless compression and lossy compression
- Different image file formats
- Different types of color spaces
- Advanced image concepts

H. Singh, *Practical Machine Learning and Image Processing*,
https://doi.org/10.1007/978-1-4842-4149-3_2

Images

Visual representation of a real-life object (a person or any other object) in a two-dimensional form is called an *image*. An image is nothing but a collection of pixels in different color spaces. Figure 2-1 is an example of a normal image.

Figure 2-1. *Normal Image*

Pixels

You might think of a complete image as a set that consists of small samples. These samples are called *pixels*. They are the smallest elements in any digital image. Have you ever zoomed in on an image to such an extent that you see small squares? Those are pixels. So, pixels are subsamples of an image that, when get combined, give us the complete image. Figure 2-2 shows how pixels, with various colors, may look.

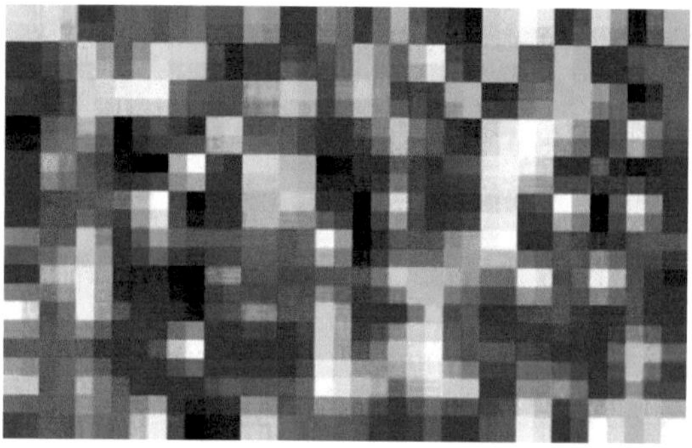

Figure 2-2. *Pixels of various colors (Source:* `www.freeimages.co.uk`*)*

Image Resolution

Image resolution is the number of pixels present in an image. The greater the number of pixels, the better quality. Image resolutions are described, for example, as 320 × 240, 640 × 480, 800 × 600, 1024 × 768, and so on. This means, for example, that there are 1024 pixel columns and 768 pixel rows. The total number of pixels is obtained by multiplying both numbers, which gives us 786,432 pixels. Figure 2-3 shows comparative depictions of different image resolutions.

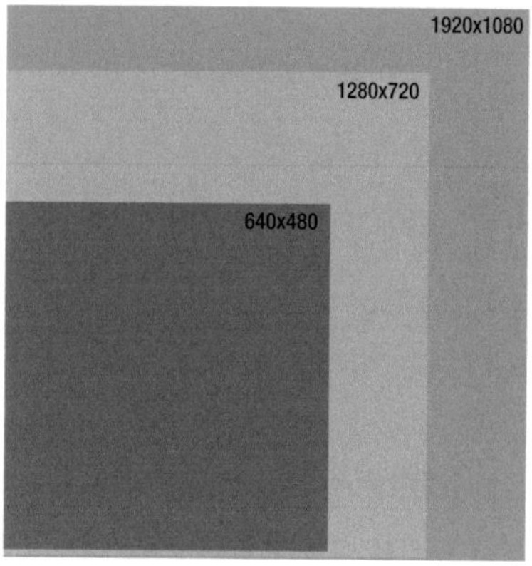

Figure 2-3. *Comparative image resolution (Source:* `www.freeimages.co.uk`*)*

PPI and DPI

As noted at the beginning of the chapter, PPI means “pixels per inch” whereas DPI means “dots per inch.” They are the units for measuring image resolution.

If we consider an inch of an image, the number of square pixels we are able to see inside it is represented by PPI. DPI, on the other hand, is related to printing. When we print an image and look at an inch of the print, the number of dots of ink used is represented by DPI.

As shown in Figure 2-4, PPI looks more smooth whereas DPI is crispier.

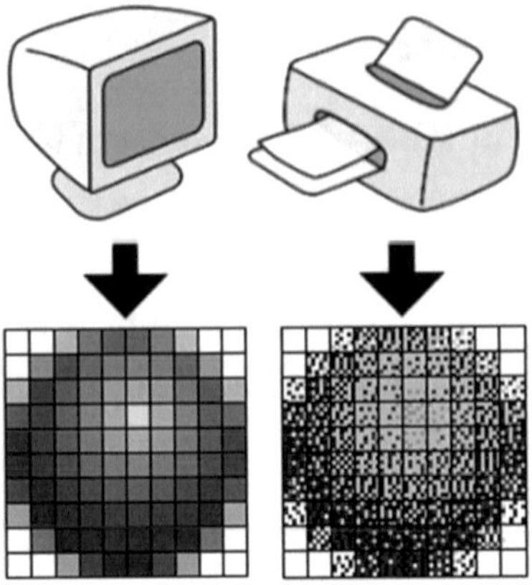

Figure 2-4. *PPI and DPI representations*

Bitmap Images

In general, when we look at pixel values, they are a range of integers. But, when we convert the range of integers into bytes, we then have a bitmap image.

One kind of bitmap is a binary image in which each pixel has one of two numbers: either a zero or a one. They represent black or white and are often used for storing images efficiently. Figure 2-5 shows a binary bitmap image.

Figure 2-5. *Binary bitmap Representation of Figure 2-1*

Lossless Compression

When we want to reduce the size of a file (which can be an image), but we don't want to compromise quality, this kind of compression is called a *lossless compression*. The compressed file can be saved, but when we require it, during the decompression process, all the information is restored and we get the actual image (Figure 2-6). This first type of compression gives priority to the information contained in the file—especially when compressing text, where we cannot afford to lose even a single piece of information.

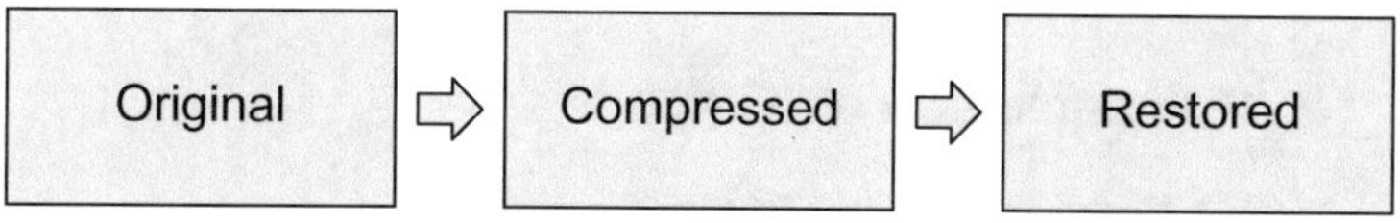

Figure 2-6. *Lossless compression process*

Lossy Compression

With lossy compression, on the other hand, some of the data may be lost. Lossy compression prioritizes saving space, rather than the accuracy of the retrieved file. Some files, such as those that contain music or images, can be trimmed and still be unaffected by the compression. There may be some loss, but it isn't worrisome (Figure 2-7).

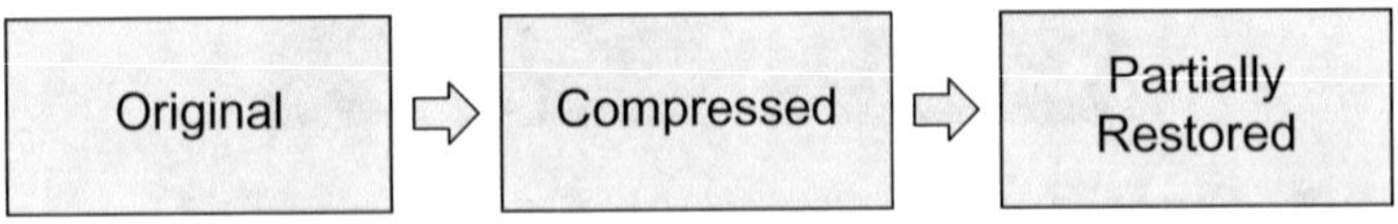

Figure 2-7. *Lossy compression process*

Image File Formats

The following are some of the most widely used image formats, which are explained in Table 2-1:

- *JPEG*: Joint Photographic Experts Group
- *JPEG2000*: New JPEG format developed in 2000
- *TIFF*: Tagged Image File Format
- *GIF*: Graphics Interchange Format
- *BMP*: Bitmap
- *PNG*: Portable Network Graphics
- *WebP*: Format developed by Google
- *SVG*: Scalable Vector Graphics

Table 2-1. *Descriptions and Uses of Different Image Types*

Image Format	Description	Use
JPEG	Lossy compression of raw images	Photographs and paintings
JPEG2000	Optimized form of JPEG; better compression ratio; both lossless and lossy compression	Surveillance
TIFF	Lossless compression; can be stored and retrieved without losing information	Document storage
GIF	Bitmap image format; supports animation; lossless compression	Gaming and animation
BMP	Independent of display device; lacks of compression	In Windows
PNG	Lossless data compression; supports different color spaces	Image transfer over the Internet
WebP	Lossless and lossy compression; small size, but comparable image quality with JPEG	Stickers in messaging apps
SVG	For interactivity and animation; behaviors and images defined in XML format; they can be searched, indexed, and compressed	Web site development

Color Spaces

The organization of the colors of in an image in a specific format is called *color space*. The way in which a color is represented is called a *color model*. Each and every image uses one of the following color spaces for effective picture representation:

- *RGB*: red, green, blue
- *XYZ*: color in the x, y, and z dimensions

- *HSV/HSL*: hue, saturation, and value/hue, saturation, and lightness
- *LAB*: luminance, and green–red and blue–yellow color components
- *LCH*: lightness, chroma, and hue
- *YPbPr*: green, blue, and red cables
- *YUV*: brightness and chroma, or color
- *YIQ*: luminance, in-phase parameter, and quadrature

Let's have a look at all these color models one by one.

RGB

Using the RGB color space, red, green, and blue are mixed in different ways to make different color combinations. Why do we use RGB? Because our eyes have color receptors that can perceive these three colors and their combinations quite effectively.

We can form any color, theoretically, from these three colors. Each color's intensity is defined within a range of 0 to 255. This range is called *color depth*.

RGB color space has two more components :

1. White point chromaticity
2. Gamma connection curve

Figure 2-8 shows a Venn diagram of the RGB color space.

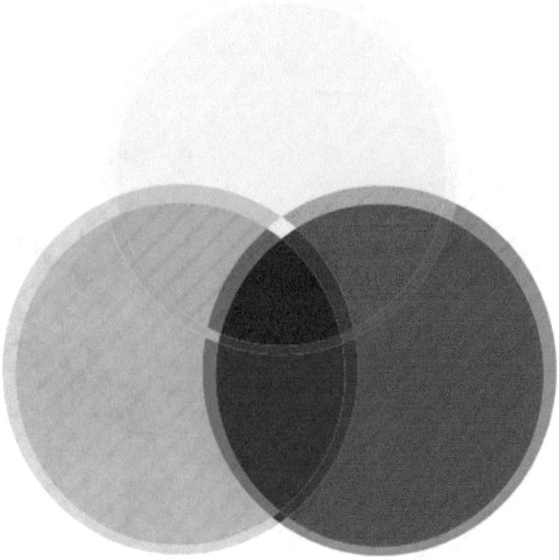

Figure 2-8. *RGB colors overlap*

XYZ

RGB colors have a threshold of saturation. They cannot go beyond what we can see. The XYZ color space helps us go beyond this threshold. Now, you may wonder why we would want to go beyond the threshold. Well, it may not be possible for our human eyes to perceive certain colors, but in the digital world, you may need these colors to be used. For example, XYZ can be used for color matching; we can enter a color code and then reproduce later it in different application, such as printing. Using XYZ, we can encode all the colors that exist in the real world. This color space is called *XYZ* because it extrapolates RGB colors in three dimensions: x, y, and z. Figure 2-9 presents an XYZ representation of an image.

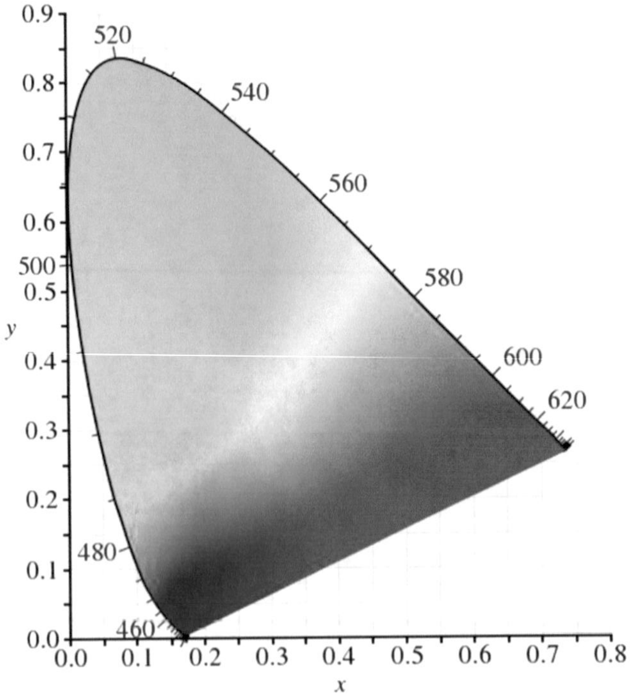

Figure 2-9. *The XYZ color space*

Pixel Thresholding A threshold is used for establishing conditions. For example, if a pixel intensity is greater than 47, make it black or make it white; 47 is called a *threshold*.

Extrapolation If we predict or estimate some value based upon its relationship with previous values, we are extrapolating. A neighbor to white pixel may be white (by assumption or extrapolation).

HSV/HSL

HSV/HSL is an alternative representation of the RGB color space. It consists of the following components:

- Hue
- Saturation
- Value
- Lightness

Hue is a property that describes three colors: green, red, and magenta. It can also be a mixture of two pure colors: red and yellow, and yellow and green

Saturation measures the intensity of an image. It tells us how far a color is from gray. A lower value means the color is approaching gray.

Lightness refers to the intensity of color with respect to white. It tells us how far a color is from white.

Value is another measure of intensity. It tells us how far a color is from black. Figure 2-10 shows an HSV representation of an image

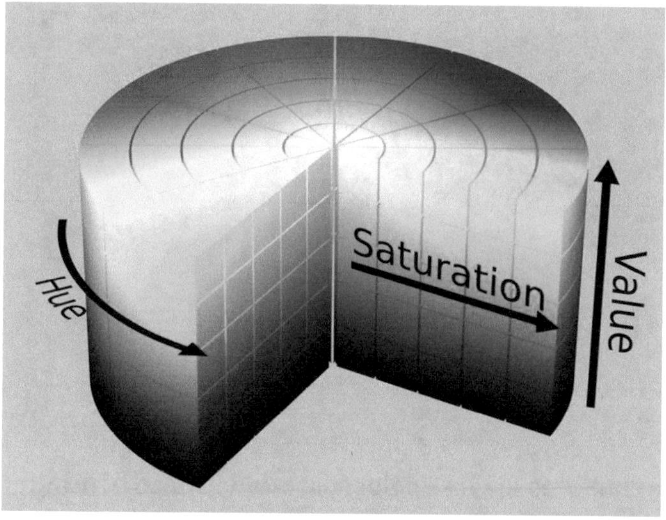

Figure 2-10. *The HSV color space*

LAB

The LAB color space has three components:

1. Luminance
2. a*, which is the green and red color component
3. b*, which is the blue and yellow color component

The colors we can perceive, and those we cannot, are included in the LAB color space. Humans are able to perceive a point, with set coordinates, and the distance to a point. Together a point and the distance to it has *cylindrical coordinates*. Anything that does not have cylindrical coordinates cannot be perceived by humans. The best part about the LAB color space is that it is not device dependent; it can be used in printing, textiles, and a host of other applications. The LAB color space is one of the most exact means of representing a color. Figure 2-11 shows a LAB representation of an image.

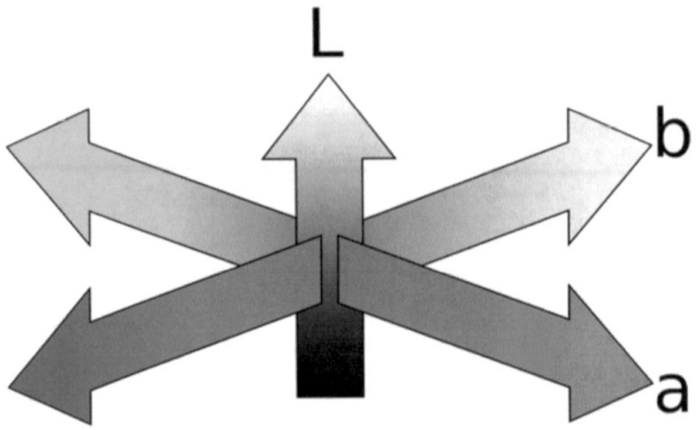

Figure 2-11. *The LAB color space*

LCH

The LCH is similar to the LAB color space, but instead of using cylindrical coordinates, it uses rectangular coordinates. This makes the coordinates similar to how our human eye sees, which is, describing a point based on not only its positional coordinates, but also by the distance from a reference point. Hence it makes it ideal for human eye perception, since the reference point in this case is our eyes.

YPbPr

The YPbPr color space is used in video electronics, such as DVD players. It consists of following three components:

1. *Y*: the green cable
2. *Pb*: the blue cable
3. *Pr*: the red cable

The three components are derived from the RGB color space only. Y refers to brightness; Pb and Pr are the two different color signals. In general, when using computers, the digital color components are derived from the RGB color space. However, when we talk about electronic devices (such as DVD players), we need to use the analog counterpart of the RGB color space, which is YPbPr. Figure 2-12 shows a standard YPbPr cable.

Figure 2-12. *YPbPr cables*

YUV

The YUV color space is somewhat similar to YPbPr, because both are used in video electronics. The difference is that YUV supports black-and-white television as well.

- *Y*: the brightness present in an image. Its value can range from 0 to 255.
- *U and V*: the chroma, or color, component. Its value can range from –128 to +127 (in the case of signed integers) or from 0 to 255 (in the case of unsigned integers).

If we remove the U and V component, we get a grayscale image. U and V are color matrices (Figure 2-13).

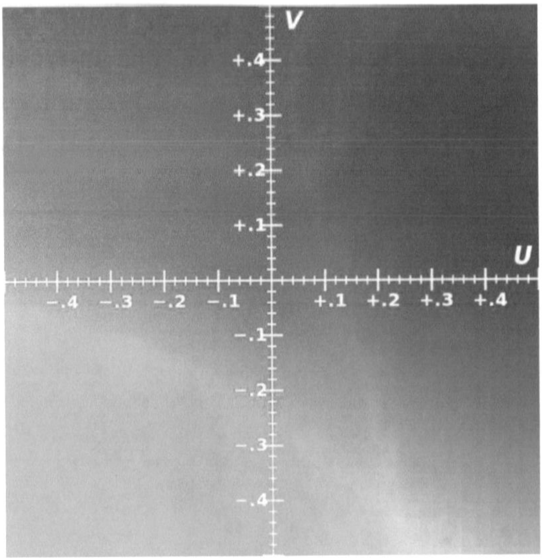

Figure 2-13. *The YUV color space*

YIQ

The YIQ color space (Figure 2-14) is used in color televisions (the NTSC mode: National Television System Committee). It consists of following three components:

1. *Y*: the luminance in an image
2. *I*: the in-phase parameter
3. *Q*: the quadrature representing the color information

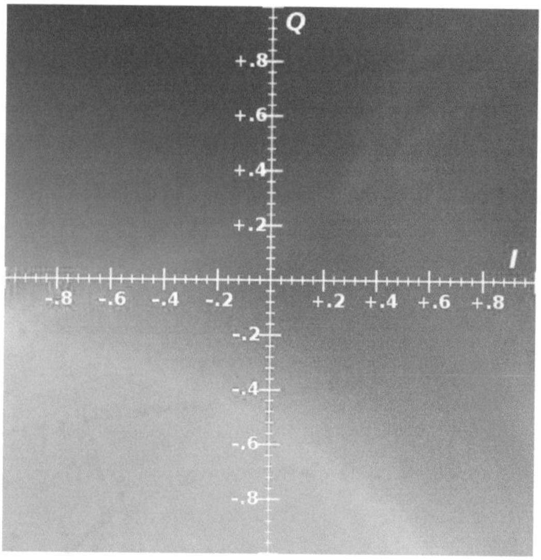

Figure 2-14. *The YIQ color space*

Advanced Image Concepts

Now that we have examined at some of the basic concepts related to color, let's look at terminology and concepts related to image processing:

- Bezier curve
- Ellipsoid
- Gamma correction

- Structural Similarity Index
- Deconvolution
- Homography
- Convolution

Bezier Curve

The Bezier curve is a curve that has numerous control points. Control points are a few select points on a canvas that we can use to adjust the curve. As we change the position of the control points, the shape of the curve changes and it is used for manipulating frames and motion. It can also be used to zoom, select the position of an image, change or transform part of an image, and more. Figure 2-15 shows a normal Bezier curve.

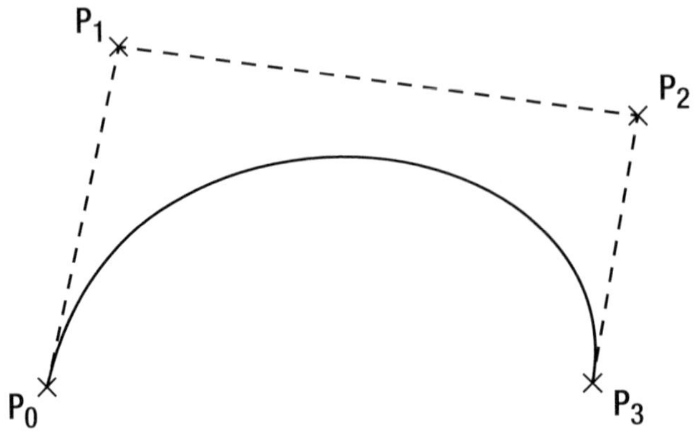

***Figure 2-15.** Bezier curve and control points*

Ellipsoid

A circle is a two-dimensional figure with a constant diameter or radius. A sphere is a three-dimensional circle that also has a constant radius or diameter. But, if we take a sphere and squash it on two sides, it becomes an ellipsoid.

Ellipsoids don't have constant diameters. One side has a larger diameter and is called the *major axis*; the smaller side is called the *minor axis*. Figure 2-16 shows a sphere and two ellipsoids.

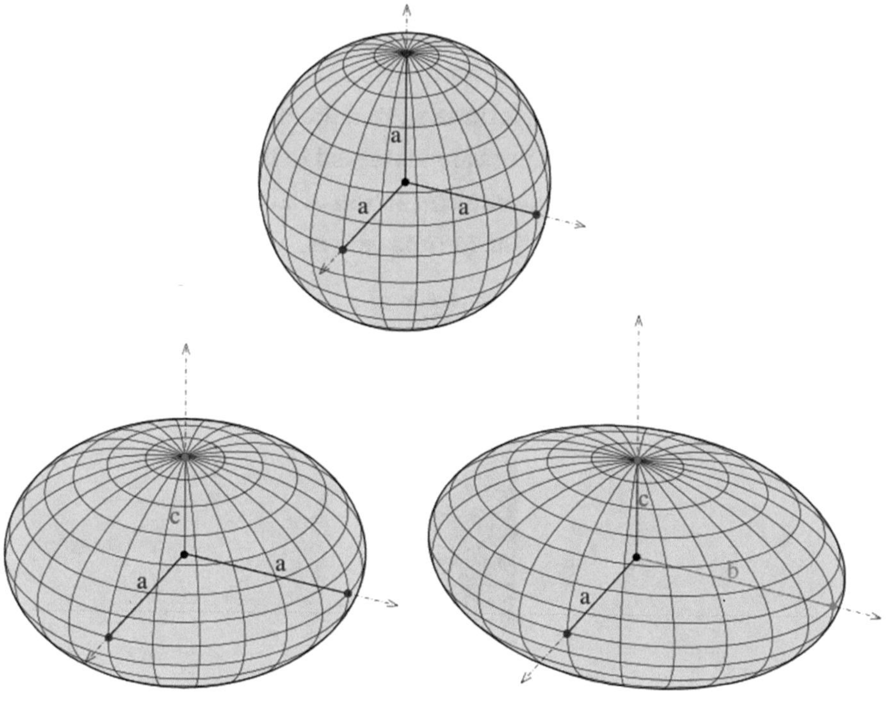

Figure 2-16. *A sphere compared with two ellipsoids*

Gamma Correction

Gamma correction, which is used to display an image accurately onscreen, controls the brightness of an image and can be used to change the red-to-green-to-blue ratio.

If there is a pixel we want to display at a particular intensity (for example, x), and the computer screen has a gamma value of 2.5, the pixel intensity on a computer monitor becomes $x^{2.5}$. Because intensity is always measured between zero to one, the image on the monitor in this case becomes fuzzy.

To eliminate this problem, the input value should be gamma-corrected. Gamma connection is done so that the output is almost similar to input. For example, if the input value is raised to the power 1/2.5, then this process is referred to as gamma correction of 2.5. Figure 2-17 shows how an image looks with different gamma values.

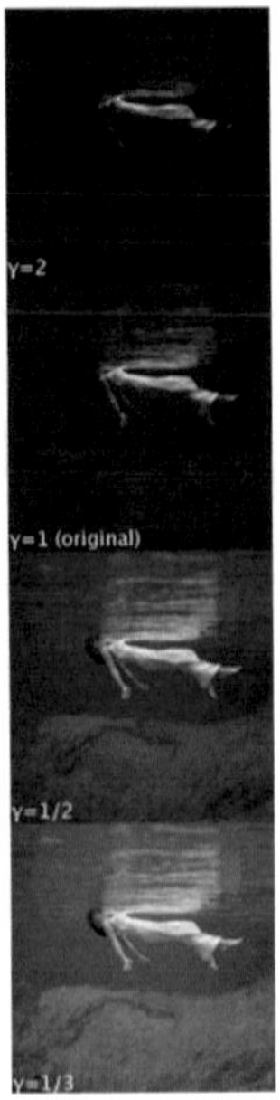

***Figure 2-17.** Gamma correction of an image using different values*

Structural Similarity Index

The Structural Similarity Index, or SSIM, is used for measuring the quality of an image. It tells how much one image is structurally similar to other, which means we need two images to perform the SSIM calculation. One constraint here is that we must know which image is the original; otherwise, the algorithm cannot differentiate between which image is better than other. The SSIM formula is

$$ssim(x,y) = (2\mu_x\mu_y + c_1) \times (2\sigma_{xy} + c_2) / (\mu_x^2+\mu_y^2 + c_2)(\sigma_x^2 + \sigma_y^2 + c_2),$$

where μ is the mean of images, σ is the standard deviation of the images, and σ^2 is the variance of the images.

SSIM(x,y) should be equal to SSIM(y,x). That's the similarity condition.

Deconvolution

In general, deconvolution is used to correct blurry images, which helps restore contrast. With blurred images, it is difficult to determine pixel intensity. To make this correction, we use what is called the *point spread function* (PSF). We select a point inside an image and, using the PSF, we can represent that point with a pattern of light (emitted from that point) in a three-dimensional, which helps make the image clearer. Figure 2-18 shows a deconvolved lunar image.

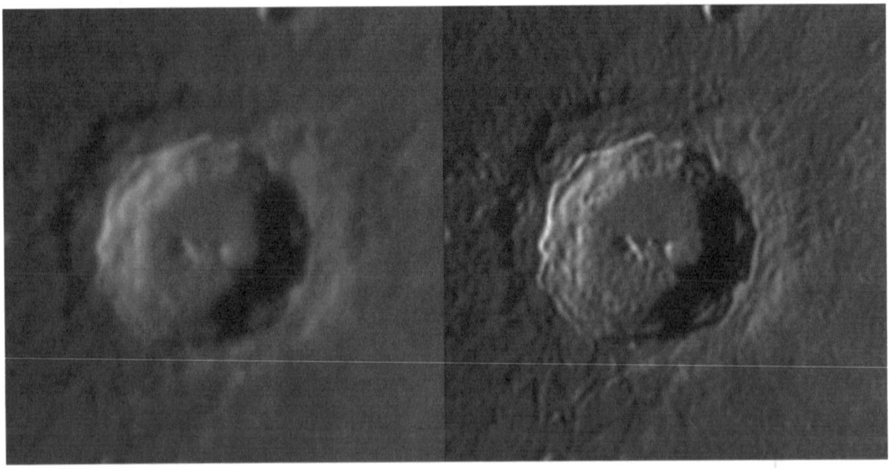

Figure 2-18. *Deconvolution of a lunar image*

Suppose we capture an image in bad weather conditions. Because of the abnormal light conditions, the contrast of the image may not be ideal. We use contrast restoration to adjust the image contrast to obtain a better picture. Under the process of Contrast Restoration nearby pixels are analyzed, and other parameters are also considered, like depth of the picture, structure of it, etc. and then using them deconvolution defines the best contrast for an image.

Homography

Homography has multiple uses in image processing: the generation of mosaic and panoramic images, image stitching, image registration, image alignment, and more. It is used to transform an image from one projective plane to another. Hence, it can be used to change the plane and the perspective of an image. Apart from the x and y coordinates of the image (which results in a flat, two-dimensional image), a third dimension is added: z. Figure 2-19 shows the same point after homography is applied, resulting in a changed perspective.

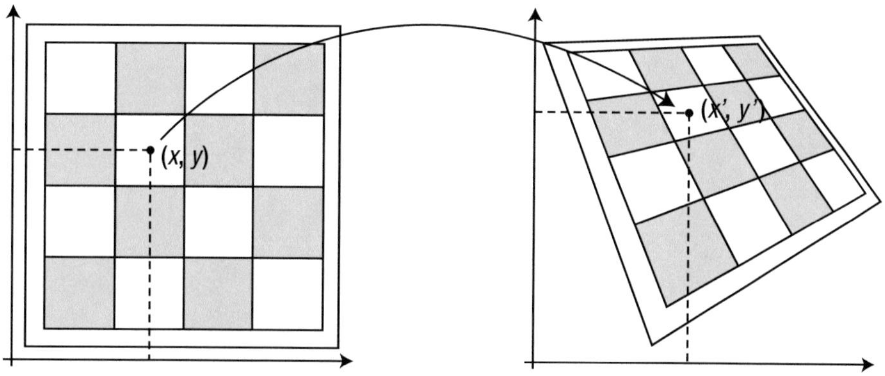

Figure 2-19. *Homography application to change the perspective of an image*

Convolution

Convolution is a simple process during which we apply a matrix (also called a *kernel* or a *filter*) to an image so that we can downsize it, or add several padding layers to keep the size the same. Convolution is also used to extract specific features from an image, such as a shape, an edge, and so on. Convolution is used in a lot in image processing, especially in convolutional neural networks and facial detection. We will talk about Convolution in detail in Chapter 6.

Next, in Chapter 3, we examine basic Python concepts and implement some of the concepts discussed in this chapter by writing Python scripts.

CHAPTER 3

Basics of Python and Scikit Image

Doing image processing without using a programing language is like counting the number of stars as you stare at the night sky. There are so many complex methodologies that, even if we try to do it manually, it's not at all possible. But, if we use programing languages such as Python, R, C++, MATLAB, and so on, the same work can be done in a jiffy.

The thing is, we should know the language before we start applying any of the image processing methods. This chapter aims at helping you achieve both goals. The first half of the chapter deals with the basic concepts of Python that are useful in applying image processing techniques. The second half of the chapter looks at the Python's image processing library: Scikit Learn. All the concepts we studied in the previous chapter, along with a few others, can be applied in Python using Scikit Learn. By the end of this chapter, you should feel comfortable with Python concepts and basic image processing applications.

H. Singh, *Practical Machine Learning and Image Processing*,
https://doi.org/10.1007/978-1-4842-4149-3_3

Basics of Python

In this section we briefly examine the following concepts:

- Variables and data types
- Data structures
- Control flow statements
- Conditional Statements
- Functions

Variables and Data Types

The first thing we need to understand about Python is how to save the data and in which format the data should be saved. We need to set our imaging variables as a container, inside which we store the data. If we don't use the variables, we may be able to do computations, but we will not be able to save our output. Let's look at an example:

```
name = 'Saurav'
age = 20
height = 6.5
```

In this example, `name`, `age`, and `height` are the variables that store the values Saurav, 20, and 6.5, respectively. There are few rules we need to follow when naming a variable:

- Variables names must start with a letter or an underscore.
- The rest of the variable name may consist of letters, numbers, and underscores.
- Names are case sensitive.
- We must not use Python built-in names.

Now we need to look at data types. In the previous example, we stored three kinds of data: text, which is enclosed single quotes; an integer, and a value with a decimal. Python knows automatically that anything enclosed between quotes is String, anything without a decimal is Int, and anything with decimal is Float. These are the three kinds of data types in Python.

Now that we know how to save a value inside a variable, we may require to print it. Printing can be done as

```
name = 'Saurav'
age = 20
height = 6.5
print(name,age,height)
```

```
Output: 20,6.5
```

or as

```
name = 'Saurav'
age = 20
height = 6.5
print(name)
print(age)
print(height)
```

```
Output:
Saurav
20
6.5
```

or as

```
name = 'Saurav'
age = 20
height = 6.5
print("the name is", name)
```

```
print("the age is", age)
print("the height is", height)
```

```
Output:
the name is Saurav'
the age is 20
the height is 6.5
```

Another way of printing is to use connectors:

```
name = 'Saurav'
age = 20
height = 6.5
print("My name is %s. My age and height is %d, %f" %(name, age,
height))
```

```
Output:
My name is Saurav'. My age and height is 20, 6.5
```

In the previous example, %s represents String, where "s" stands for string; %d represents Int, where "d" stands for digit or integer; and %f represents decimals, where "f" stands for float. So, the first connector is connected to first variable, the second to the second, and the third to the third. Everything is joined using "%" (Figure 3-1).

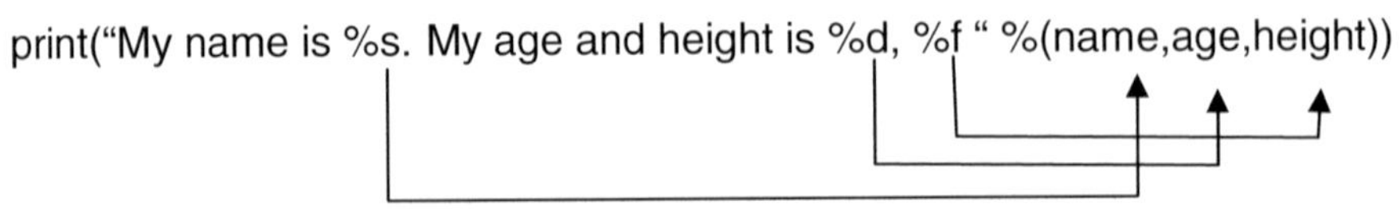

***Figure 3-1.** How connectors work*

Data Structures

In the previous section, we saw how to save one value inside a variable. But, if we want to save more than one value, then we must use Python data structures, which include the following:

- Lists
- Dictionaries
- Tuples

These structures are the ones most widely used in image processing.

Lists

We can use lists to store multiple values inside a single variable. For example,

```
Age = [24,35,26,42]
Names = ["Sachin","Saurav","Rahul"]
```

As you can see, the lists always start and end with square brackets.

Dictionaries

Dictionaries are combinations of keys and values. Just as a regular dictionary has words and meanings, you can think of keys and values as words and meanings. For example,

```
Details ={"Sachin":24, "Saurav":35, "Rahul":42}
```

Dictionaries always start and end with curly braces. Also, the keys and values are separated by a colon. First element before the colon is the key; the element after the colon is the value.

Tuples

Tuples also store values in a manner similar to lists. The difference is that tuples are immutable—meaning, once a tuple is defined, the values cannot be modified. Tuples start and end with parenthesis. For example,

```
Height = (6.5, 5.4, 5.11)
```

Control Flow Statements

There are two kinds of control flow statements:

1. a `while` loop
2. a `for` loop

If we want to repeat a particular operation several times, we use control flow statements. Suppose we want to generate a multiplication table of two. Let's look at how we can do this using a `while` loop and a `for` loop.

```
count = 1
while count<=10:
 table = 2*count
 count = count+1
 print table
Output:
2
4
6
8
10
12
14
16
18
20
```

Let's examine the syntax of a `while` loop. Figure 3-2 depicts the functioning of a `while` loop.

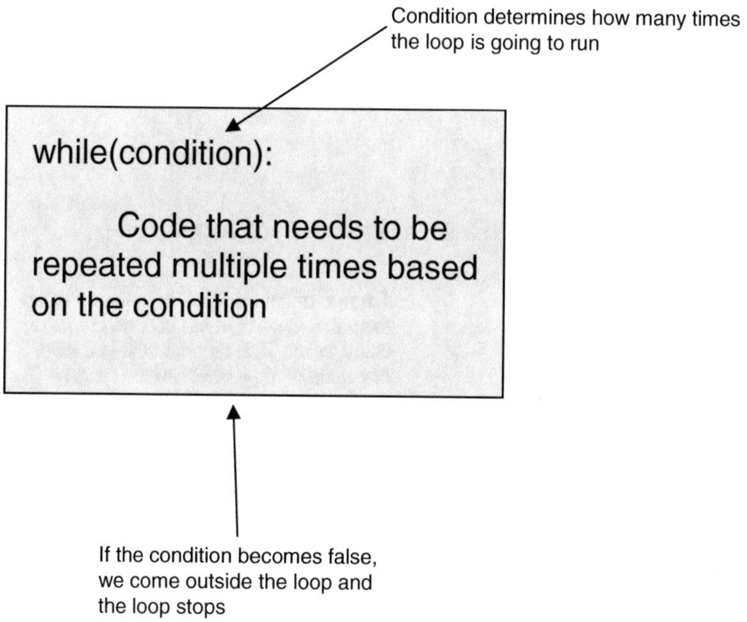
Condition determines how many times the loop is going to run
while(condition):
Code that needs to be repeated multiple times based on the condition
If the condition becomes false, we come outside the loop and the loop stops

Figure 3-2. *How a* `while` *loop works*

The loop in our code snippet will run ten times, because we inserted the condition of less than or equal to ten. When the count hits 11, the condition fails and we come out of the loop.

Now let's look at how we can use `for` loop for the same problem.

```
for i in range(10):
 table=2*(i+1)
 print(table)
Output:
2
4
6
```

```
8
10
12
14
16
18
20
```

Figure 3-3 depicts the functioning of the `for` loop.

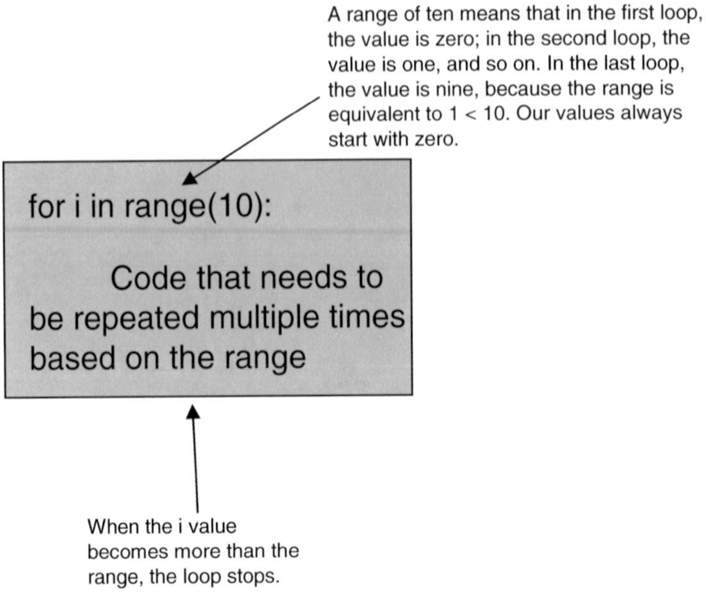
A range of ten means that in the first loop, the value is zero; in the second loop, the value is one, and so on. In the last loop, the value is nine, because the range is equivalent to 1 < 10. Our values always start with zero.
for i in range(10):
Code that needs to be repeated multiple times based on the range
When the i value becomes more than the range, the loop stops.

Figure 3-3. *How a `for` loop works*

The `for` loop in our example will run ten times because we have stipulated a range of 10. When the value of i equals ten, the loop stops.

We use `while` loops when we want conditions-based looping; we use `for` loops when we have predefined numbers. Both the loops are very important in the field of image processing, as you will see later.

Conditional Statements

Conditional statements are used to give a binary result based on a condition that you provide. All the conditions discussed in Table 3-1 can be used in the following example. If the result is true or 1, then the code block inside the conditional statement gets executed; otherwise, it does not. Conditional statements can be of the following types:

- `if`
- `if-else`
- `if-elif-else`

Table 3-1. *Conditional Operators*

Condition	Meaning
`a == b`	Checks if a is equal to b
`a != b`	Checks if a is not equal to b
`a < b`	Checks if a is less than b
`a <= b`	Checks if a is less than and equal to b
`a > b`	Checks if a is greater than b
`a >= b`	Checks if a is greater than and equal to b

Let's look at all the three with one example. Suppose we want to give an A to students who got more than 80 points on a test, a B to those who got more than 60 points and less than 80 points, and a C to those students who got 59 points or less. Here is the code:

```
marks = 45
if marks >= 80:
 print("You got A Grade")
elif marks >=60 and marks <80:
```

```
 print("You got B Grade")
else:
 print("You got C Grade")
Output:
You got C Grade
```

This code executes one by one. First, the variable `marks` is assigned a value of 45. Then the first conditional statement is encountered. If the value of `marks` is greater than or equal to 80, an A grade is assigned. If not this is not the case, the `elif` statement is encountered, which checks for the second condition. If none of the conditions are true, the student is assigned a C.

Functions

Functions are used when you want to enclose complex codes inside a single wrapper, and then use that wrapper multiple times without writing the code again and again. It's like we dedicate a jar for containing sugar, and whenever we want to take out sugar, we use that jar only, not the bag in which you have sugar along with salt, veggies, and snacks.

Figure 3-4 describes functions in a nutshell. A function can take one or more values as inputs—I1, I2, I3, and so on (In)—and gives one or more results as an output (O).

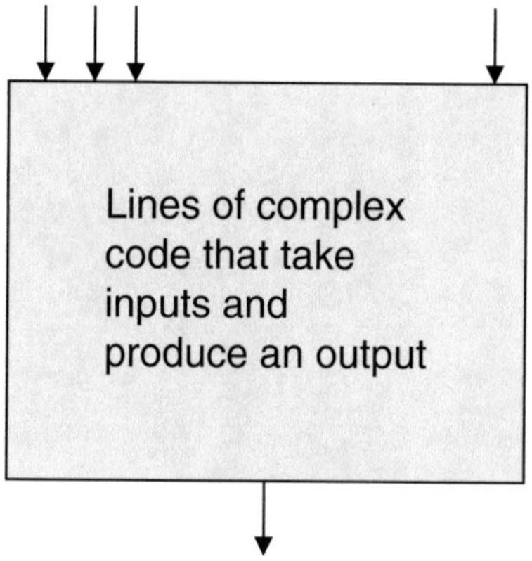

Figure 3-4. *How a function works*

Let's look at how to use functions based on the following example. Up until now, we've generated a multiplication table of two using `for` and `while` loops, but suppose we want to generate a table of whatever number we want? Here's the code to do just that:

```
def table (a):
    for i in range(10):
        table = a*(i+1)
        print(table)
```

The function takes a as an input and generates a table of whatever value a stores. Let's see how to call the function. Suppose we want to generate a multiplication table of 10 and 17. We call the function:

```
table(10)
Output:
10
20
30
40
50
```

```
60
70
80
90
100
table(17)
Output:
17
34
51
68
85
102
119
136
153
170
```

Now that you've been exposed to the basics of Python, let's move on to a discussion of Scikit Image.

Scikit Image

Scikit Image is a module that is used to do basic image processing. Before we start, let's look at the definition of a module. A module is a collection of Python files, classes, or functions. We can save complex and lengthy code inside different files. To do this, we need to import the files and use them in our environment. First we need to import Scikit Image into our environment, like so:

```
import skimage
```

This single line of code imports an entire collection of classes and functions needed to do basic image analysis.

We can apply all the concepts we looked at in Chapter 2 using Scikit Image.

In this section we look at following operations using Scikit Image and Python:

- Uploading and Viewing an Image
- Getting Image Resolution
- Looking at Pixel Values
- Converting Color Space
- Saving an Image
- Creating Basic Drawings
- Doing Gamma Correction
- Rotating, Shifting, and Scaling Images
- Determining Structural Similarity

Uploading and Viewing an Image

Let's see how we can import an image into the Python environment and view it there. We start by importing a module named `skimage`, which contains different image processing algorithms. To upload and view the image, we use a class from the `skimage` module called `io`. Inside this class, we use the `imread` function to upload and read an image; the function `imshow` is used to view the image. Let's have a look at the code.

```
from skimage import io
img = io.imread('puppy.jpg')
io.imshow(img)
```

Output:

```
<matplotlib.image.AxesImage at 0x2980d6edda0>
```

Getting Image Resolution

To get the resolution of the image, we use a built-in function called shape. When an image is read, all the pixel values are stored in an array format; this array is called a *numpy array*. After we read the image and convert it to array, we use the shape function to look at the resolution.

In the following code, you can see that we have an image with a resolution of 1536 × 2048, and it has three channels (because it is in the RGB color format).

```
#Getting Image Resolution
from skimage import io
img = io.imread('puppy.jpg')
img.shape
Output:
(1536, 2048, 3)
```

Looking at Pixel Values

Now that we know the resolution of the image, we may want to look at each pixel value. To do this, we save the numpy array in one line—in other words, we use one row to store all the pixel values. When you look at he code that follows, you can see we are importing another module named `pandas`. Pandas is used to read, write, and process various file formats. Here, we save the pixel values in the Excel format:

```
#Getting Pixel Values
from skimage import io
import pandas as pd
img = io.imread('puppy.jpg')
df = pd.DataFrame(img.flatten())
filepath = 'pixel_values1.xlsx'
df.to_excel(filepath, index=False)
```

When we look at the importing line—`import pandas as pd`—it means we are renaming the imported module to `pd`. The `flatten` function is used to convert the three dimensions of an RGB image to a single dimension. We then save that image in an excel file named `pixel_values.xlsx`. To do this, we use the Pandas function called `to_excel`. The `DataFrame` function converts a one-dimensional array into an Excel-like format, with rows and columns. You can print the `df` variable to look at the data frame structure.

Converting Color Space

Suppose our image is in the RGB color space. We may want to convert it to different color formats, as discussed in Chapter 2. In this section we look at different conversions, then convert the image back to its original RGB format.

Before looking at the code, we must examine the functions we will use. For converting an image into different color formats, we need to use the class `color`, which is present in `skimage` module. Inside this class, we can use the following functions:

- `rgb2hsv`
- `hsv2rgb`
- `rgb2xyz`
- `xyz2rgb`
- `rgb2grey`
- `grey2rgb`
- `rgb2yuv`
- `yuv2rgb`
- `rgb2lab`
- `lab2rgb`
- `rgb2yiq`
- `yiq2rgb`
- `rgb2ypbpr`
- `ypbpr2rgb`

Also, we have to use one more module, called `pylab`. We import all the classes present inside `pylab` by using *. We use `pylab` to see different figures in different blocks. Then we use the function `figure` to display more than one image at a go. Let's now look at all the code and its output.

RGB to HSV and Vice Versa

```
#Import libraries
from skimage import io
from skimage import color
from skimage import data
from pylab import *
#Read image
img = io.imread('puppy.jpg')

#Convert to HSV
img_hsv = color.rgb2hsv(img)

#Convert back to RGB
img_rgb = color.hsv2rgb(img_hsv)

#Show both figures
figure(0)
```

```
io.imshow(img_hsv)
figure(1)
io.imshow(img_rgb)
```

Output:

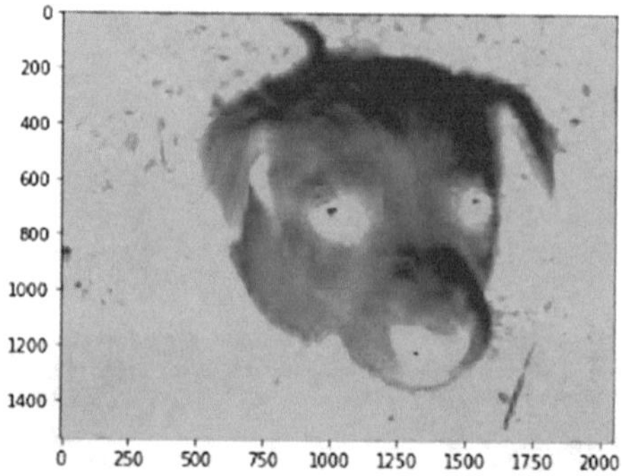

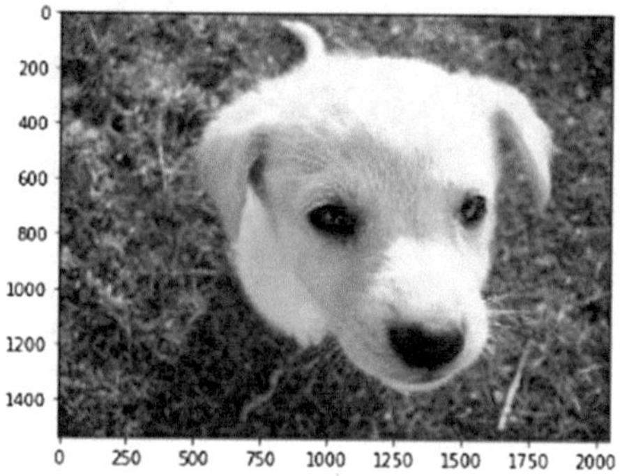

RGB to XYZ and Vice Versa

```
#Import libraries
from skimage import io
from skimage import color
from skimage import data
#Read image
img = io.imread('puppy.jpg')

#Convert to XYZ
img_xyz = color.rgb2xyz(img)
```

```
#Convert back to RGB
img_rgb = color.xyz2rgb(img_xyz)

#Show both figures
figure(0)
io.imshow(img_xyz)
figure(1)
io.imshow(img_rgb)
```

Output:

RGB to LAB and Vice Versa

```
#Import libraries
from skimage import io
from skimage import color
#Read image
img = io.imread('puppy.jpg')

#Convert to LAB
img_lab = color.rgb2lab(img)

#Convert back to RGB
img_rgb = color.lab2rgb(img_lab)

#Show both figures
figure(0)
io.imshow(img_lab)
figure(1)
io.imshow(img_rgb)
```

Output:

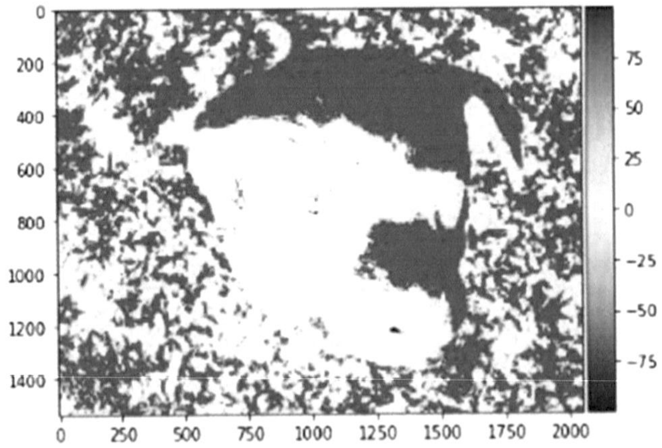

RGB to YUV and Vice Versa

```
#Import libraries
from skimage import io
from skimage import color
#Read image
img = io.imread('puppy.jpg')

#Convert to YUV
img_yuv = color.rgb2yuv(img)
```

```
#Convert back to RGB
img_rgb = color.yuv2rgb(img_yuv)

#Show both figures
figure(0)
io.imshow(img_yuv)
figure(1)
io.imshow(img_rgb)
```

Output:

RGB to YIQ and Vice Versa

```
#Import libraries
from skimage import io
from skimage import color
#Read image
img = io.imread('puppy.jpg')

#Convert to YIQ
img_yiq = color.rgb2yiq(img)

#Convert back to RGB
img_rgb = color.yiq2rgb(img_yiq)

#Show both figures
figure(0)
io.imshow(img_yiq)
figure(1)
io.imshow(img_rgb)
```

Output:

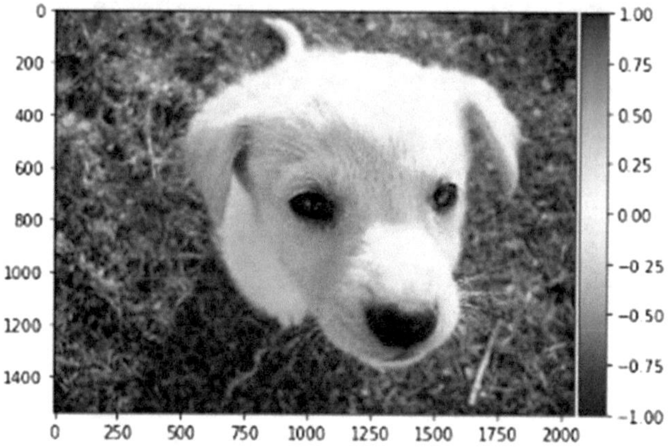

RGB to YPbPr and Vice Versa

```
#Import libraries
from skimage import io
from skimage import color
#Read image
img = io.imread('puppy.jpg')

#Convert to YPbPr
img_ypbpr= color.rgb2ypbpr(img)
```

```
#Convert back to RGB
img_rgb= color.ypbpr2rgb(img_ypbpr)

#Show both figures
figure(0)
io.imshow(img_ypbpr)
figure(1)
io.imshow(img_rgb)
```

Output:

Saving an Image

After every image analysis, we may want to save the image. To do this, we use the skimage io function called imsave. In the following code, the first argument includes the name of the file to which you want to save the image; the second is the variable that contains the image.

```
#Import libraries
from skimage import io
from skimage import color
from pylab import *
#Read image
img = io.imread('puppy.jpg')

#Convert to YPbPr
img_ypbpr= color.rgb2ypbpr(img)

#Convert back to RGB
img_rgb= color.ypbpr2rgb(img_ypbpr)

io.imsave("puppy_ypbpr.jpg", img_ypbpr)
```

Creating Basic Drawings

Within an image, we might like to draw certain figures. These figures can be simple, such as a line, or complex, such as an ellipsoid. Let's look at some basic drawings using the skimage drawing class called draw.

Lines

The line function is used to draw a simple line on an image. In the following code, the first two parameters indicate the first point; the last two parameters indicate the second point. A line is then drawn using these points. We can then change the pixel values of the line so we are able to see the line on the image.

```
from skimage import io
from skimage import draw

img = io.imread('puppy.jpg')
x,y = draw.line(0,0,1000,1000)
img[x, y] = 0
io.imshow(img)
```

Output:

```
<matplotlib.image.AxesImage at 0x298163d1128>
```

Rectangles

To draw rectangles, we use the function polygon. We can draw not only rectangle, but any kind of polygon we want. All we have to do is give x and y coordinates, then define the width and the height.

In the following code, I use the function rectangle. It returns a shape with pixel values that we change, as in the previous example of a line.

```
from skimage import io
from skimage import draw

img = io.imread('puppy.jpg')
def rectangle(x, y, w, h):
 rr, cc = [x, x + w, x + w, x], [y, y, y + h, y + h]
```

```
 return (draw.polygon(rr, cc))
rr, cc = rectangle(10, 10, 500,500)
img[rr, cc] = 1
io.imshow(img)
```

Output:

```
<matplotlib.image.AxesImage at 0x2981649dac8>
```

Circles

The `circle` function is used to draw a circle. In the following code, the first two arguments indicate the position of the circle inside the image; the last argument indicates the radius.

```
#Import libraries
from skimage import io
from skimage import draw

#Load image
img = io.imread('puppy.jpg')

#Define circle coordinates and radius
x, y = draw.circle(500,500, 100)

#Draw circle
img[x, y] = 1
```

```
#Show image
io.imshow(img)
```

Output:

```
<matplotlib.image.AxesImage at 0x298165cada0>
```

Bezier Curve

To draw a Bezier curve, we using the function `bezier_curve`. We need to indicate the position of three or more control points that then shape the curve. The first six arguments in the following code define three points; the last argument defines the tension present in the line. Play with different values change the curve.

```
#Import libraries
from skimage import io
from skimage import draw

#Load image
img = io.imread('puppy.jpg')

#Define Bezier curve coordinates
x, y = draw.bezier_curve(0,0, 500, 500, 900,1200,100)
#Draw Bezier curve
img[x, y] = 1
```

```
#Show image
io.imshow(img)
```

Output:

```
<matplotlib.image.AxesImage at 0x29817a28080>
```

Doing Gamma Correction

To perform gamma correction of an image, based on the display instrument, we use `exposure` class in `skimage`. The `exposure` class contains a function called `adjust_gamma`, which we use to give an image as an input and the final gamma value that we want. In this way, we get a gamma-corrected image.

```
from skimage import exposure
from skimage import io
from pylab import *
img = io.imread('puppy.jpg')
gamma_corrected1 = exposure.adjust_gamma(img, 0.5)
gamma_corrected2 = exposure.adjust_gamma(img, 5)
figure(0)
io.imshow(gamma_corrected1)
figure(1)
```

```
io.imshow(gamma_corrected2)
```

Output:

Rotating, Shifting, and Scaling Images

Sometimes we may want to rotate an image or change its size. To do this, we use the `transform` class in the `skimage` module. `transform` has two functions: `rotate` and `resize`. `rotate` takes the degree of rotation as its parameter; `resize` takes the new size as its parameter.

```
from skimage import io
from skimage.transform import rotate
img = io.imread('puppy.jpg')
img_rot = rotate(img, 20)
io.imshow(img_rot)
```

Output:

```
<matplotlib.image.AxesImage at 0x29817b23550>
```

```
from skimage import io
from skimage.transform import resize
img = io.imread('puppy.jpg')
img_res = resize(img, (100,100))
io.imshow(img_res)
io.imsave("ss.jpg", img_res)
```

Output:

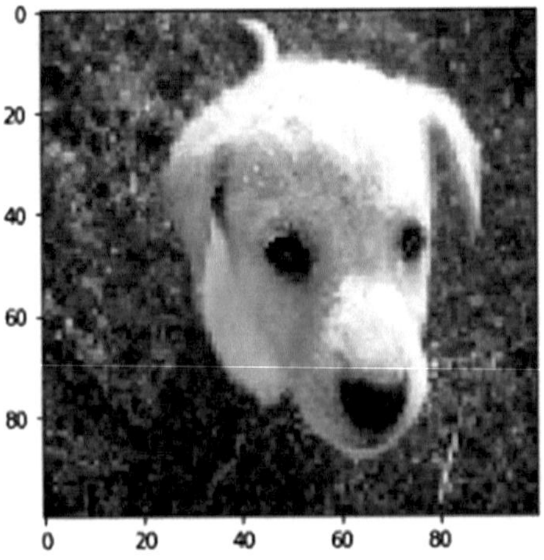

Determining Structural Similarity

As I explained earlier, structural similarity is used to find the index that indicate how much two images are similar. A value closer to one means the images are very similar; a value closer to zero means they are less similar. In the following code, for the first comparison of similar images, we get a SSIM output of 1.0. In the second bit of code, in which we compare the image with its YPbPr counterpart, we get a SSIM out of 0.43, which indicates less similarity.

```
from skimage import io
from skimage.measure import compare_ssim as ssim
img_original = io.imread('puppy.jpg')
img_modified = io.imread('puppy_ypbpr.jpg')

ssim_original = ssim(img_original, img_original, data_range=img_
original.max() - img_original.min(), multichannel=True)
ssim_different = ssim(img_original, img_modified, data_range=img_
modified.max() - img_modified.min(), multichannel=True)
print(ssim_original,ssim_different)
```

```
Output:
1.0 0.4348875243670361
```

SSIM takes three arguments. The first refers to the image; the second indicates the range of the pixels (the highest pixel color value less the lowest pixel color value). The third argument is `multichannel`. A True value means the image contains more than one channel, such as RGB. False means there is only one channel, such as grayscale.

In the next chapter we look at advanced image processing concepts using a computer vision library called OpenCV.

CHAPTER 4

Advanced Image Processing Using OpenCV

Now that we have looked at the basic image processing techniques using the Scikit Image library, we can move on to its more advanced aspects. In this chapter, we use one of the most comprehensive computer vision libraries: OpenCV and examine the following concepts:

- Blending two images
- Changing the contrast and brightness of an image
- Adding text to images
- Smoothing images
- Changing the shape of images
- Effecting image thresholding
- Calculating gradients to detect edges
- Performing histogram equalization

H. Singh, *Practical Machine Learning and Image Processing*,
https://doi.org/10.1007/978-1-4842-4149-3_4

Blending Two Images

Suppose you have two images and you want to blend them so that features of both images are visible. We use image registration techniques to blend one image over the second one and determine whether there are any changes. Let's look at the code:

```
#import required packages
import cv2

#Read image 1
img1 = cv2.imread('cat_1.jpg')
#Read image 2
img2 = cv2.imread('cat_2.jpg')

#Define alpha and beta
alpha = 0.30
beta = 0.70

#Blend images
final_image = cv2.addWeighted(img1, alpha, img2, beta, 0.0)

#Show image
io.imshow(final_image)
```

Let's look at some of the functions used in this code:

- `import cv2`: The complete OpenCV library is present in the package cv2. In Chapter 1, we learned how to install OpenCV. Now all we need to do is import this package to use the classes and functions stored in it.
- `cv2.imread()`: Similar to `skimage.io.imread()`, we have `cv2.imread()`, which is used to read the image from a particular destination.

- `cv2.addWeighted()`: This function blends the two images. The alpha and beta parameters indicate the transparency in both images. There are a few formulas that help to determine the final blending. The last parameter is called *gamma*. Currently it has a value of zero. It's just a scalar, which is added to the formulas, to transform the images more effectively. In general, gamma is zero.
- `cv2.imshow()`: Similar to `skimage.io.imshow()`, `cv2.imshow()`helps to display the image in a new window.
- `cv2.waitKey(): waitKey()` is used so that the window displaying the output remains until we click Close or press Escape. If we do not include this function after `cv2.imshow()`, the images are not displayed.
- `cv2.DestroyAllWindows()`: After we have clicked Close or pressed Escape, this function destroys all the windows that have been opened and saved in the memory.

The following pictures are the output of the previous code:

Changing Contrast and Brightness

To change contrast and brightness in an image, we should have an understanding of what these two terms mean:

- *Contrast*: Contrast is the difference between maximum and minimum pixel intensity.
- *Brightness*: Brightness refers to the lightness or darkness of an image. To make an image brighter, we add a constant number to all the pixels present in it.

Let's look at the code and the output, to see the difference between contrast and brightness.

```
#import required packages
import cv2
import numpy as np

#Read image
image = cv2.imread("cat_1.jpg")

#Create a dummy image that stores different contrast and
brightness
new_image = np.zeros(image.shape, image.dtype)

#Brightness and contrast parameters
contrast = 3.0
bright = 2

#Change the contrast and brightness
for y in range(image.shape[0]):
    for x in range(image.shape[1]):
        for c in range(image.shape[2]):
            new_image[y,x,c] = np.clip(contrast*image[y,x,c] +
            bright, 0, 255)
```

```
figure(0)
io.imshow(image)
figure(1)
io.imshow(new_image)
```

In this code, we did not use any `cv2` functions to change the brightness or contrast. We used the numpy library and a slicing concept to change the parameters. The first thing we did was define the parameters. We gave contrast a value of 3 and brightness a value of 2. The first `for` loop gave the image width, the second gave the image height, and the third gave the image channels. Therefore, the first loop runs width a number of times, the second loop runs height a number of times, and the last loop runs the number of color channels a number of times. If the RGB image is there, then loop runs three times for the three channels.

`np.clip()` limits the values in a particular range. In the previous code, the range is 0 to 255, which is nothing but the pixel values for each channel. So, a formula is derived:

$$(\text{Specific pixel value} \times \text{Contrast}) + \text{Brightness}.$$

Using the this formula, we can change each and every pixel value, and `np.clip()` makes sure the output value doesn't go beyond 0 to 255. Hence, the loops traverse through each and every pixel, for each and every channel, and does the transformation.

Here is are the output images:

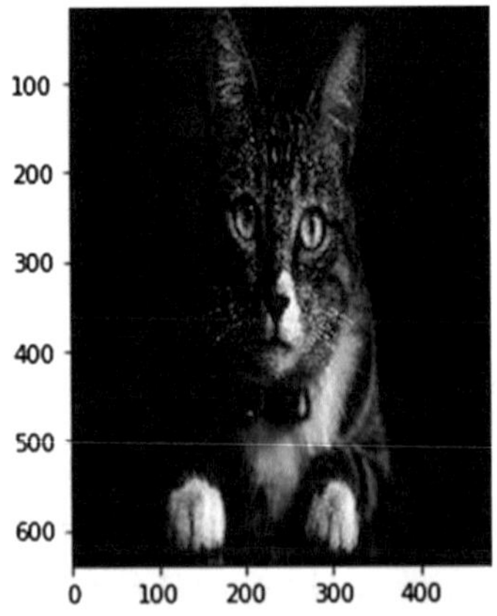

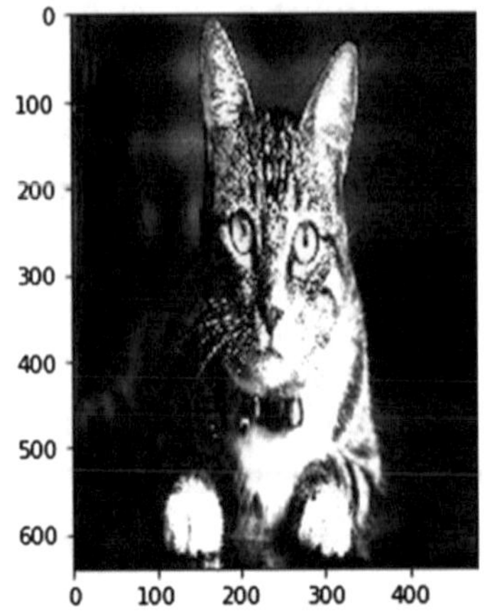

Adding Text to Images

`cv2.putText()` is a function present in the `cv2` module that allows us to add text to images. The function takes following arguments:

- Image, where you want to write the text
- The text you want to write
- Position of the text on the image

- Font type
- Font scale
- Color of the text
- Thickness of text
- Type of line used

As you can see in the code that follows, the font used is FONT_HERSHEY_SIMPLEX. cv2 also supports following fonts:

- FONT_HERSHEY_SIMPLEX
- FONT_HERSHEY_PLAIN
- FONT_HERSHEY_DUPLEX
- FONT_HERSHEY_COMPLEX
- FONT_HERSHEY_TRIPLEX
- FONT_HERSHEY_COMPLEX_SMALL
- FONT_HERSHEY_SCRIPT_SIMPLEX
- FONT_HERSHEY_SCRIPT_COMPLEX
- FONT_ITALIC

The type of line that used in the code is cv2.LINE_AA. Other types of lines that are supported are

- FILLED: a completely filled line
- LINE_4: four connected lines
- LINE_8: eight connected lines
- LINE_AA: an anti-aliasing line

You can experiment using all the different arguments and check the results. Let's look at the code and its output.

```
#import required packages
import cv2
import numpy as np

#Read image
image = cv2.imread("cat_1.jpg")

#Define font
font  = cv2.FONT_HERSHEY_SIMPLEX

#Write on the image
cv2.putText(image, "I am a Cat", (230, 50), font, 0.8, (0, 255, 0),
2, cv2.LINE_AA)

io.imshow(image)
```

Output:

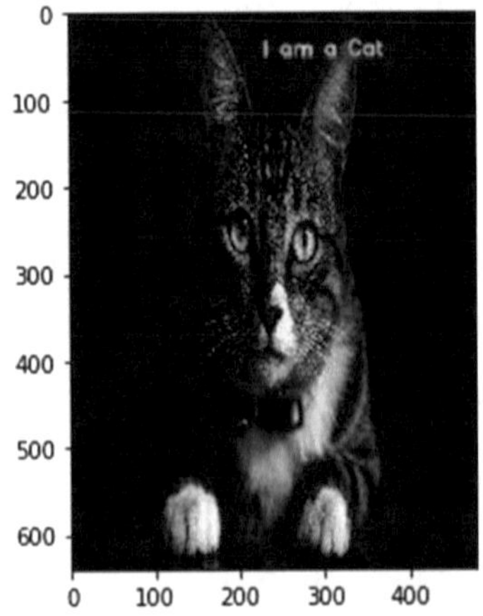

Smoothing Images

In this section we take a look at three filters used to smooth images. These filters are as follows:

- The median filter (`cv2.medianBlur`)
- The gaussian filter (`cv2.GaussianBlur`)
- The bilateral filter (`cv2.bilateralFilter`)

Median Filter

The median filter is one of the most basic image-smoothing filters. It's a nonlinear filter that removes black-and-white noise present in an image by finding the median using neighboring pixels.

To smooth an image using the median filter, we look at the first 3 × 3 matrix, find the median of that matrix, then remove the central value by that median. Next, we move one step to the right and repeat this process until all the pixels have been covered. The final image is a smoothed image. If you want to preserve the edges of your image while blurring, the median filter is your best option.

`cv2.medianBlur` is the function used to achieve median blur. It has two parameters:

1. The image we want to smooth
2. The kernel size, which should be odd. Thus, a value of 9 means a 9 × 9 matrix.

Gaussian Filter

The gaussian filter depends on the standard deviation of the image (distribution) and assumes the mean is zero (we can define a mean different from zero as well). Gaussian filters do not take care of the edges.

Value of certain statistical parameter defines the preservation. It is used for basic image blurring. It generally works by defining a kernel. Suppose we define a 3 × 3 kernel. We apply this kernel to each and every pixel present in the image, and average the result, which results in a blurred image. Here's an example:

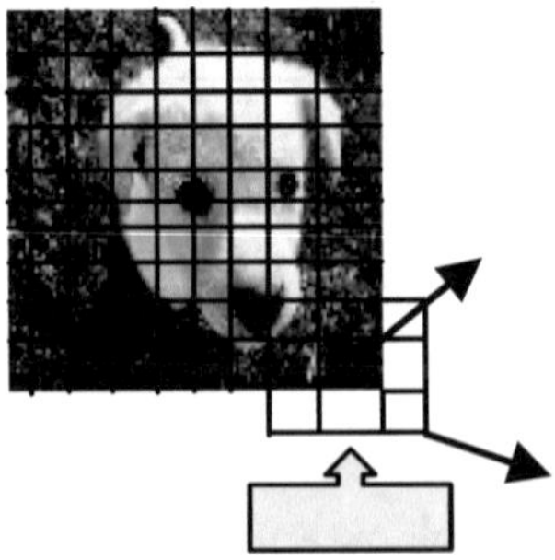

`cv2.GaussianBlur()` is the function used to apply a gaussian filter. It has three parameters:

1. The image, which needs to be blurred
2. The size of the kernel (3 × 3 in this case)
3. The standard deviation

Bilateral Filter

If we want to smooth an image and keep the edges intact, we use a bilateral filter. Its implementation is simple: We replace the pixel value with the average of its neighbors. This is a nonlinear smoothing approach that takes the weighted average of neighboring pixels. "Neighbors" are defined in following ways:

- Two pixel values are close to each other
- Two pixel values are similar to each other

`cv2.bilateralFilter` has four parameters:

1. The image we want to smooth
2. The diameter of the pixel neighborhood (defining the neighborhood diameter to search for neighbors)
3. The sigma value for color (to find the pixels that are similar)
4. The sigma value for space (to find the pixels that are closer)

Let's take a look at the code:

```
#import required packages
import cv2
import numpy as np

#Read images for different blurring purposes
image_Original = cv2.imread("cat_1.jpg")
image_MedianBlur = cv2.imread("cat_1.jpg")
image_GaussianBlur = cv2.imread("cat_1.jpg")
image_BilateralBlur = cv2.imread("cat_1.jpg")

#Blur images
image_MedianBlur=cv2.medianBlur(image_MedianBlur,9)
image_GaussianBlur=cv2.GaussianBlur(image_GaussianBlur,(9,9),10)
image_BilateralBlur=cv2.bilateralFilter(image_BilateralBlur,9,
100,75)

#Show images
figure(0)
io.imshow(image_Original)
figure(1)
io.imshow(image_MedianBlur)
figure(2)
```

```
io.imshow(image_GaussianBlur)
figure(3)
io.imshow(image_BilateralBlur)
```

Output:

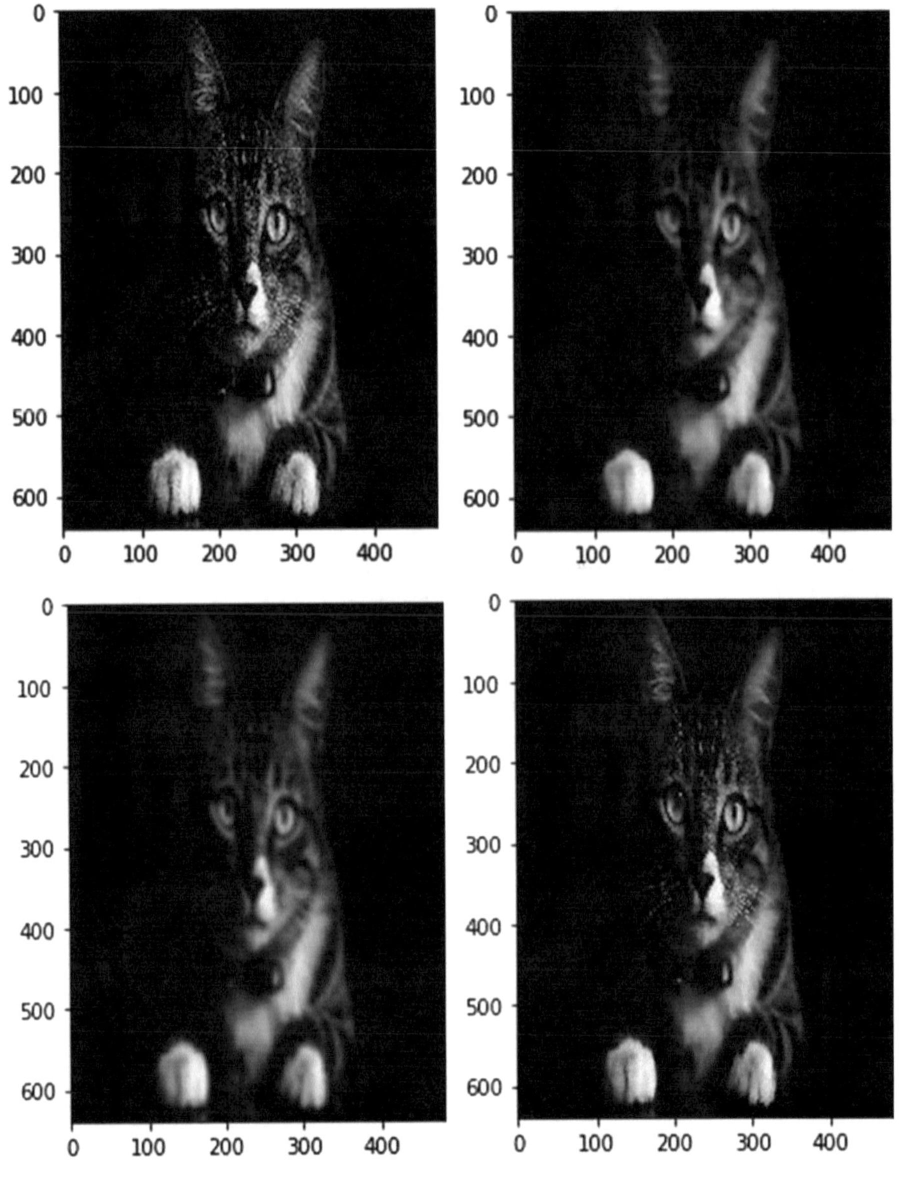

Changing the Shape of Images

In this section we examine erosion and dilation, which are the two operations used to change the shape of images. Dilation results in the addition of pixels to the boundary of an object; erosion leads to the removal of pixels from the boundary.

Two erode or dilate an image, we first define the neighborhood kernel, which can be done in three ways:

1. `MORPH_RECT`: to make a rectangular kernel
2. `MORPH_CROSS`: to make a cross-shaped kernel
3. `MORPH_ELLIPS`: to make an elliptical kernel

The kernel finds the neighbors of a pixel, which helps us in eroding or dilating an image. For dilation, the maximum value generates a new pixel value. For erosion, the minimum value in a kernel generates a new pixel value.

In Figure 4-1, we apply a 3 × 1 matrix to find the minimum for each row. For the first element, the kernel starts from one cell before. Because the value is not present in the new cell to the left, we take it as blank. This concept is called *padding*. So, the first minimum is checked between none, 141 and 157. Thus, 141 is the minimum, and you see 141 as the first value in the right matrix. Then, the kernel shifts toward right. Now the cells to consider are 141, 157, and 65. This time, 65 is the minimum, so second value in the new matrix is 65. The third time, the kernel compares 157, 65, and none, because there is no third cell. Therefore, the minimum is 65 and that becomes the last value. This operation is performed for each and every cell, and you get the new matrix shown in Figure 4-1.

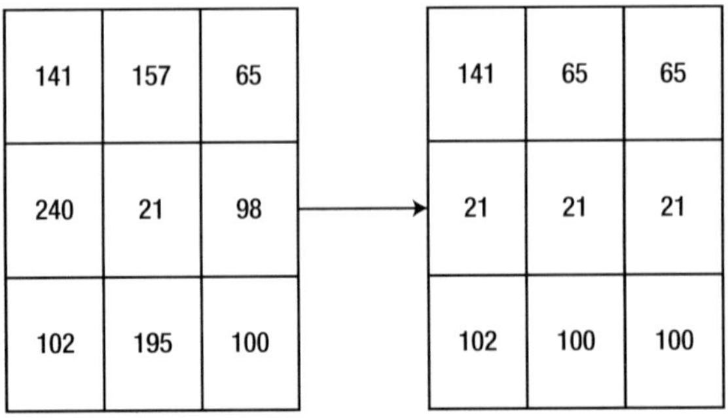

Figure 4-1. *Dilation*

The erosion operation is done similar to dilation, except instead of finding the minimum, we find the maximum. Figure 4-2 shows the operation.

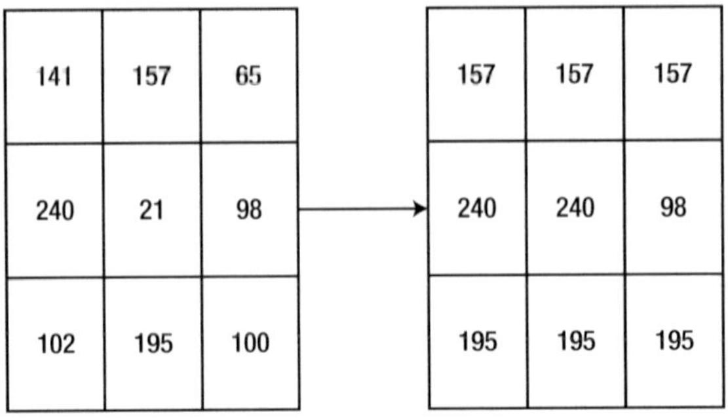

Figure 4-2. *Erosion*

The kernel size is, as in dilation, a 3 × 1 rectangle. `cv2.getStructuringElement()` is the function used to define the kernel and pass it down to the erode or dilate function. Let's see its parameters:

- Erosion/dilation type
- Kernel size
- Point at which the kernel should start

After applying cv2.getStructuringElement() and getting the final kernel, we use cv2.erode() and cv2.dilate() to perform the specific operations. Let's look at the code and its output:

```
#DILATION CODE:

#Import package
import cv2

#Read image
image = cv2.imread("cat_1.jpg")

#Define erosion size
s1 = 0
s2 = 10
s3 = 10

#Define erosion type
t1 = cv2.MORPH_RECT
t2 = cv2.MORPH_CROSS
t3 = cv2.MORPH_ELLIPSE

#Define and save the erosion template
tmp1 = cv2.getStructuringElement(t1, (2*s1 + 1, 2*s1+1), (s1, s1))
tmp2= cv2.getStructuringElement(t2, (2*s2 + 1, 2*s2+1), (s2, s2))
tmp3 = cv2.getStructuringElement(t3, (2*s3 + 1, 2*s3+1), (s3, s3))

#Apply the erosion template to the image and save in different
variables
final1 = cv2.erode(image, tmp1)
final2 = cv2.erode(image, tmp2)
final3 = cv2.erode(image, tmp3)

#Show all the images with different erosions
figure(0)
io.imshow(final1)
```

```
figure(1)
io.imshow(final2)
figure(2)
io.imshow(final3)

#EROSION CODE:

#Import packages
import cv2

#Read images
image = cv2.imread("cat_1.jpg")

#Define dilation size
d1 = 0
d2 = 10
d3 = 20

#Define dilation type
t1 = cv2.MORPH_RECT
t2 = cv2.MORPH_CROSS
t3 = cv2.MORPH_ELLIPSE

#Store the dilation templates
tmp1 = cv2.getStructuringElement(t1, (2*d1 + 1, 2*d1+1), (d1, d1))
tmp2 = cv2.getStructuringElement(t2, (2*d2 + 1, 2*d2+1), (d2, d2))
tmp3 = cv2.getStructuringElement(t3, (2*d3 + 1, 2*d3+1), (d3, d3))

#Apply dilation to the images
final1 = cv2.dilate(image, tmp1)
final2 = cv2.dilate(image, tmp2)
final3 = cv2.dilate(image, tmp3)

#Show the images
figure(0)
io.imshow(final1)
```

```
figure(1)
io.imshow(final2)
figure(2)
io.imshow(final3)
```

Output:

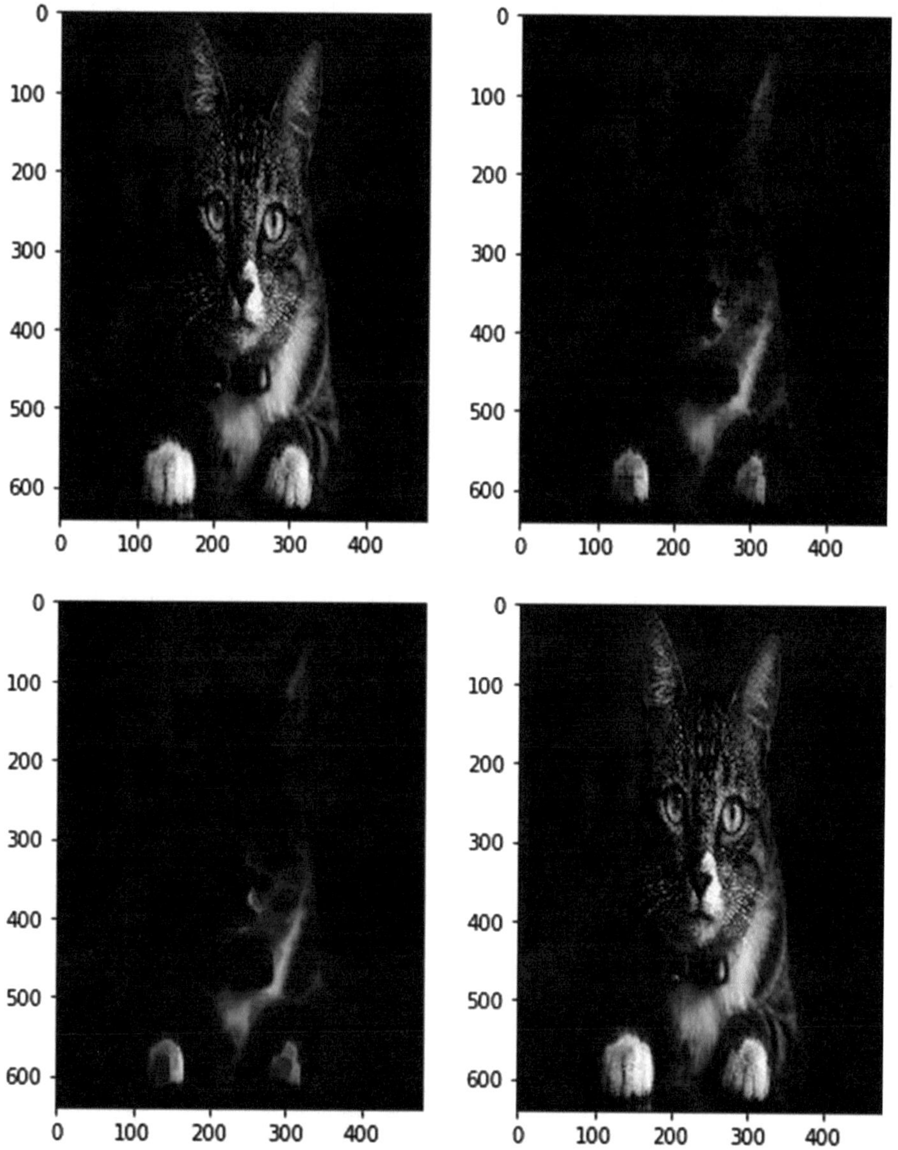

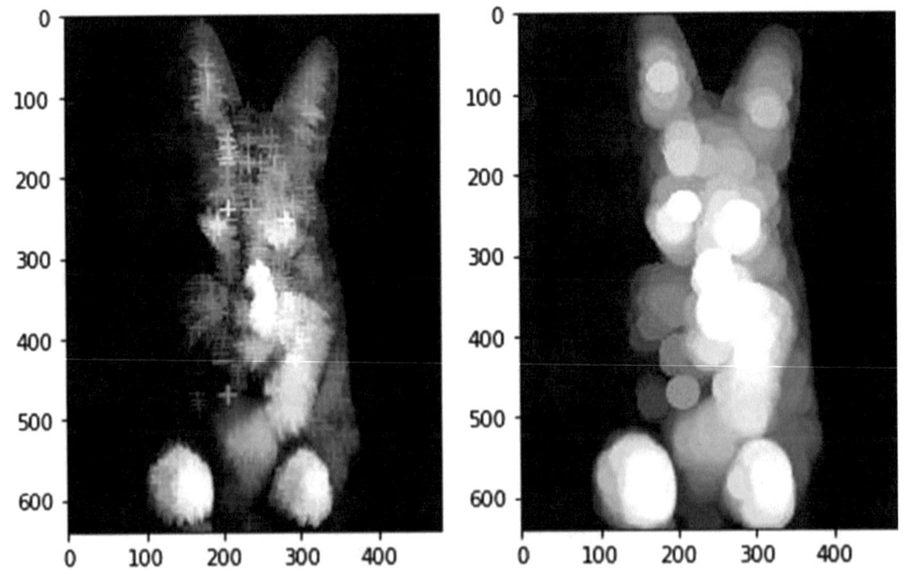

Effecting Image Thresholding

The main reason you would do image thresholding is to segment images. We try to get an object out of the image by removing the background and by focusing on the object. To do this, we first convert the image to grayscale and then into a binary format—meaning, the image contains black or white only.

We provide a reference pixel value, and all the values above or below it are converted to black or white. There are five thresholding types:

1. *Binary*: If the pixel value is greater than the reference pixel value (the threshold value), then convert to white (255); otherwise, convert to black (0).

2. *Binary inverted*: If the pixel value is greater than the reference pixel value (the threshold value), then convert to black (0); otherwise, convert to white (255). Just the opposite of the binary type.

3. *Truncated*: If the pixel value is greater than the reference pixel value (the threshold value), then convert to the threshold value; otherwise, don't change the value.

4. *Threshold to zero*: If the pixel value is greater than the reference pixel value (the threshold value), then don't change the value; otherwise convert to black (0).

5. *Threshold to zero inverted*: If the pixel value is greater than the reference pixel value (the threshold value), then convert to black (0); otherwise, don't change.

We use the `cv2.threshold()` function to do image thresholding, which uses the following parameters:

- The image to convert
- The threshold value
- The maximum pixel value
- The type of thresholding (as listed earlier)

Let's look at the code and its output.

```
#Import packages
import cv2

#Read image
image = cv2.imread("cat_1.jpg")

#Define threshold types
"'
0 - Binary
1 - Binary Inverted
```

```
2 - Truncated
3 - Threshold To Zero
4 - Threshold To Zero Inverted
'''

#Apply different thresholds and save in different variables
_, img1 = cv2.threshold(image, 50, 255, 0 )
_, img2 = cv2.threshold(image, 50, 255, 1 )
_, img3 = cv2.threshold(image, 50, 255, 2 )
_, img4 = cv2.threshold(image, 50, 255, 3 )
_, img5 = cv2.threshold(image, 50, 255, 4 )

#Show the different threshold images
figure(0)
io.imshow(img1) #Prints Binary Image
figure(1)
io.imshow(img2) #Prints Binary Inverted Image
figure(2)
io.imshow(img3) #Prints Truncated Image
figure(3)
io.imshow(img4) #Prints Threshold to Zero Image
figure(4)
io.imshow(img5) #Prints Threshold to Zero Inverted Image
```

Output:

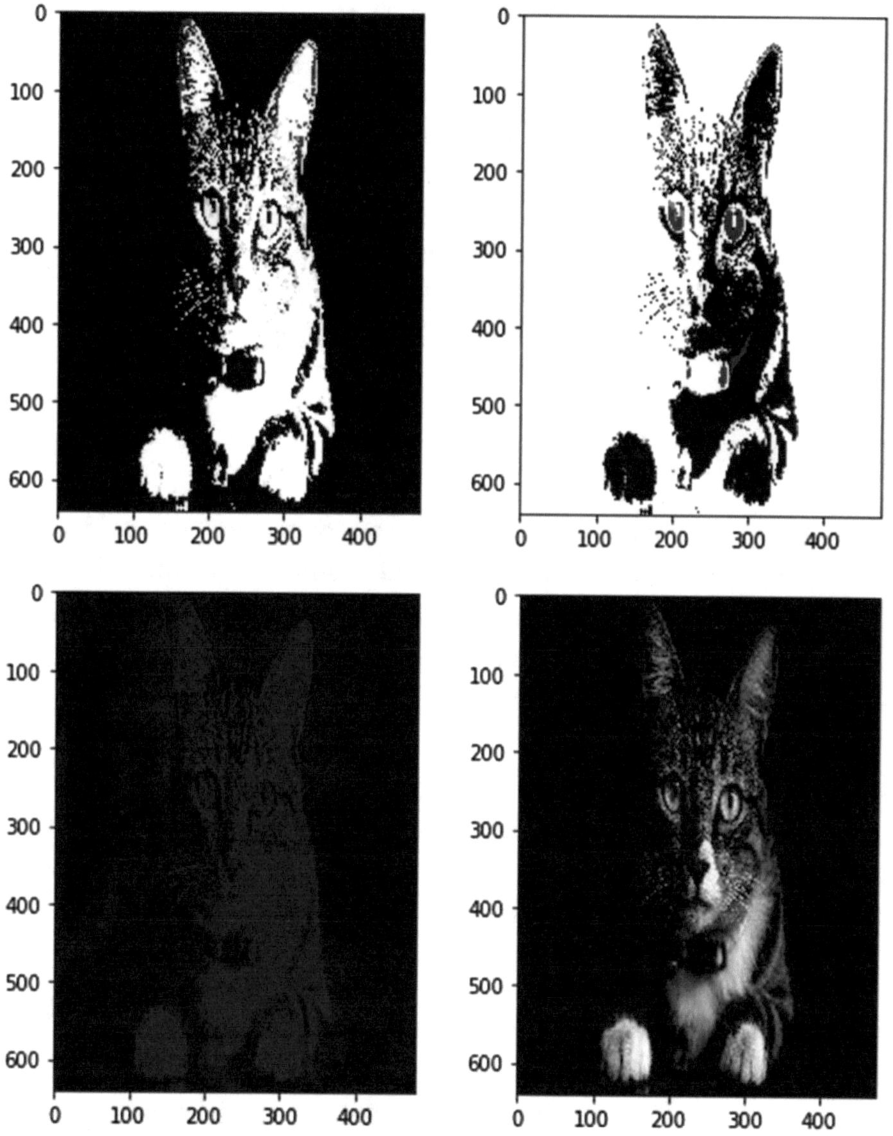

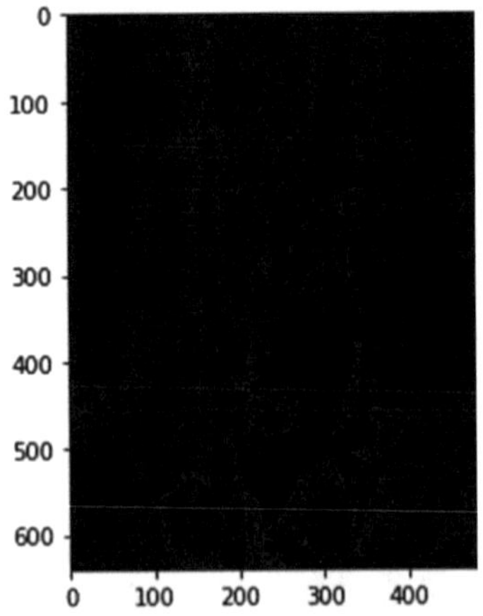

Calculating Gradients

In this section we look at edge detection using Sobel derivatives. Edges are found in two directions: the vertical direction and the horizontal direction. With this algorithm, we emphasize only those regions that have very high spatial frequency, which may correspond to edges. Spatial frequency is the level of detail present in an area of importance.

In the following code, we read the image, apply gaussian blur so the noise is removed, then convert the image to grayscale. We use the `cv2.cvtColor()` function to convert the image to grayscale. We can also use `skimage` functions to do the same. Last, we give the grayscale output to the `cv2.Sobel()` function. Let's look at Sobel Function's parameters:

- Input image
- Depth of the output image. The greater the depth of the image, the lesser the chances you miss any border. You can experiment with all of the below listed parameters, to see whether they capture the borders effectively, per your requirements. Depth can be of following types:

    - -1 (the same depth as the original image)
    - `cv2.CV_16S`
    - `cv2.CV_32F`
    - `cv2.CV_64F`
- Order of derivative x (defines the derivative order for finding horizontal edges)
- Order of derivative y (defines the derivative order for finding vertical edges)
- Size of the kernel
- Scale factor to be applied to the derivatives
- Delta value to be added as a scalar in the formula
- Border type for extrapolation of pixels

The `cv2.convertScaleAbs()` function is used to convert the values into an absolute number, with an unsigned 8-bit type. Then we blend the x and y gradients that we found to find the overall edges in the image.

Let's look at the code and its output.

```
#Import packages
import cv2

#Read image
src = cv2.imread("cat_1.jpg")

#Apply gaussian blur
cv2.GaussianBlur(src, (3, 3), 0)

#Convert image to grayscale
gray = cv2.cvtColor(src, cv2.COLOR_BGR2GRAY)
```

```
#Apply Sobel method to the grayscale image
grad_x = cv2.Sobel(gray, cv2.CV_16S, 1, 0, ksize=3, scale=1,
delta=0, borderType=cv2.BORDER_DEFAULT) #Horizontal Sobel
Derivation
grad_y = cv2.Sobel(gray, cv2.CV_16S, 0, 1, ksize=3, scale=1,
delta=0, borderType=cv2.BORDER_DEFAULT) #Vertical Sobel
Derivation
abs_grad_x = cv2.convertScaleAbs(grad_x)
abs_grad_y = cv2.convertScaleAbs(grad_y)
grad = cv2.addWeighted(abs_grad_x, 0.5, abs_grad_y, 0.5, 0)
#Apply both

#Show the image
io.imshow(grad)#View the image
```

Output:

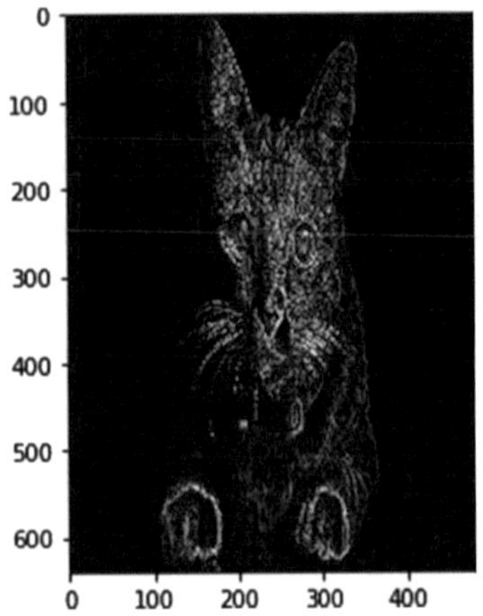

Performing Histogram Equalization

Histogram equalization is used to adjust the contrast of an image. We first plot the histogram of pixel intensity distribution and then modify it. There is a cumulative probability function associated with every image. Histogram equalization gives linear trend to that function. We should use a grayscale image to perform histogram equalization.

The `cv2.equalizeHist()` function is used for histogram equalization. Let's look at an example.

```
#Import packages
import cv2

#Read image
src = cv2.imread("cat_1.jpg")

#Convert to grayscale
src = cv2.cvtColor(src, cv2.COLOR_BGR2GRAY)

#Apply equalize histogram
src_eqlzd = cv2.equalizeHist(src) #Performs Histogram Equalization

#Show both images
figure(0)
io.imshow(src)
figure(1)
io.imshow(src_eqlzd)
figure(2)
io.imshow(src_eqlzd)
```

Output:

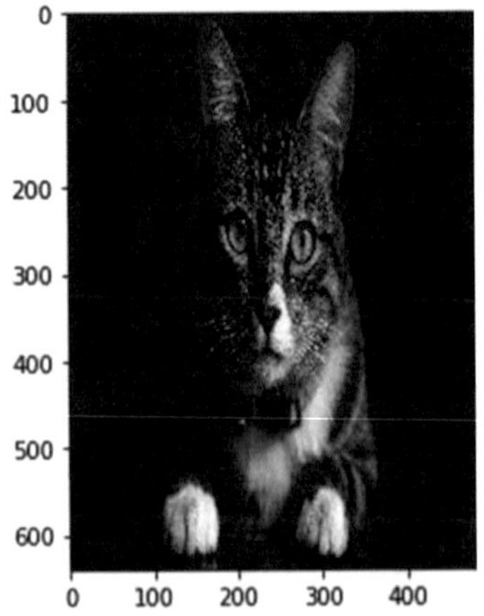

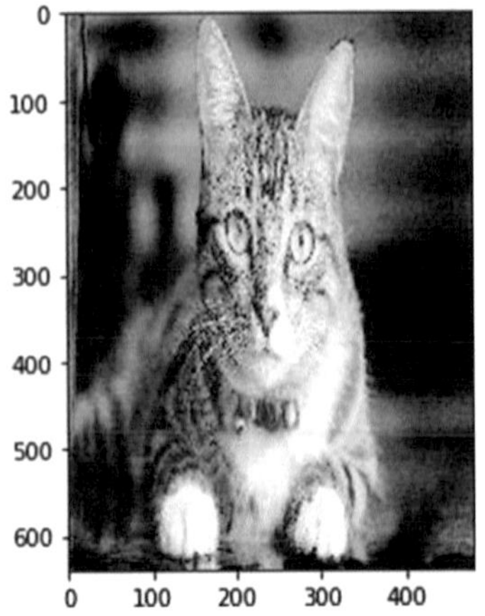

Now we know the basic image processing algorithms using `skimage`, and some of the advanced operations using OpenCV. In the next chapter, we move ahead and apply machine learning algorithms to do image processing.

CHAPTER 5

Image Processing Using Machine Learning

We start this chapter by examining a few of the most widely used image processing algorithms, then move on to machine learning implementation in image processing. The chapter at a glance is as follows:

- Feature mapping using the scale-invariant feature transform (SIFT) algorithm
- Image registration using the random sample consensus (RANSAC) algorithm
- Image Classification using artificial neural networks
- Image classification using convolutional neural networks (CNNs)
- Image Classification using machine learning
- Important Terms

H. Singh, *Practical Machine Learning and Image Processing*,
https://doi.org/10.1007/978-1-4842-4149-3_5

Feature Mapping Using the SIFT Algorithm

Suppose we have two images. One image is of a bench in a park. The second image is of the entire park, which also includes the bench. Now suppose we want to write code that helps us find the bench inside the park image. You might think this is an easy task, but let me add some complexity. What if the image of the bench is a zoomed image? Or what if it is rotated? Or both? How are you going to deal with it now?

The answer lies in the scale-invariant feature transform, or SIFT algorithm. As the name suggest, it is scale invariant, which means that no matter how much we zoom in on (or out of) the image, we can still find similarities. Another feature of this algorithm is that it is rotation invariant. Regardless of degree of rotation, it still performs well. The only issue with this algorithm is that it's patented, which means that for academic purposes it's good, but for commercial purpose there may be lot of legal issues involved with using it. However, this won't stop us from learning and applying this algorithm for now.

We first must understand the basics of the algorithm. Then we can apply it to finding similarities between two images using Python and then we'll look at the code line by line.

Let's look at the features of the image that the SIFT algorithm tries to factor out during processing:

- Scale (zoomed-in or zoomed-out image)
- Rotation
- Illumination
- Perspective

As you can see, not only are scale and rotation accommodated, the SIFT algorithm also takes care of the illumination present in the image and the perspective from which we are looking. But how does it do all of this? Let's take a look at the step-by-step process of using the SIFT algorithm:

1. Find and constructing a space to ensure scale invariance
2. Find the difference between the gaussians
3. Find the important points present inside the image
4. Remove the unimportant points to make efficient comparisons
5. Provide orientation to the important points found in step 3
6. Identifying the key features uniquely.

Step 1: Space Construction

In the first step, we take the original image and perform gaussian blurring, so that we can remove some of the unimportant points and the extra noise present in the image. When this is done, we resize the image and repeat the process. There are various factors on which resizing and blurring depend, but we won't go into the mathematical details here.

Step 2: Difference between the Gaussians

In the second step, we take the images from step 1 and find the difference between their values. This makes the image scale invariant.

Step 3: Important Points

During the third step, we identify important points (also called *key points*). The difference between the gaussians image that we found in step 3 is used to determine the local maxima and minima. We take each pixel and then check its neighbors. The pixel is marked as a key point if it is greatest (maximum) or least (minimum) among all its neighbors.

The next step is to find subpixel maxima and/or minima. We find subpixels using a mathematical concept called the *Taylor expansion*. When the subpixels are found, we then try to find the maxima and minima again, using the same process. Also, to only take corners and consider them as key points, we use a mathematical concept called the *Hessian matrix*. Corners are always considered the best key points.

Step 4: Unimportant Key Points

In this step we first determine a threshold value. In the key points-generated image, and the subpixels image, we check the pixel intensity with the threshold value. If it is less than the threshold value, we consider it an unimportant key point and reject it.

Step 5: Orientation of Key Points

We find the direction of gradient and the magnitude for each key point and its neighbors, then we look at the most prevalent orientation around the key point and assign the same to it. We use histograms to find these orientations and to get the final one.

Step 6: Key Features

To make the key points unique, we extract key features from them. Also, we make sure that while comparing these key points with the second image, they should not look exactly similar, but almost similar.

Now that we know the basics of the algorithm, let's look at the code to which algorithm is applied to a pair of images.

```
import cv2
import numpy as np
import matplotlib.pyplot as plt
from Sift_Operations import *

print("'Make Sure that both the images are in the same folder"')

x = input("Enter First Image Name: ")
Image1 = cv2.imread(x)
y = input("Enter Second Image Name: ")
Image2 = cv2.imread(y)

Image1_gray = cv2.cvtColor(Image1, cv2.COLOR_BGR2GRAY)
Image2_gray = cv2.cvtColor(Image2, cv2.COLOR_BGR2GRAY)

Image1_key_points, Image1_descriptors = extract_sift_
features(Image1_gray)
Image2_key_points, Image2_descriptors = extract_sift_
features(Image2_gray)

print( 'Displaying SIFT Features')
showing_sift_features(Image1_gray, Image1, Image1_key_points);

norm = cv2.NORM_L2
bruteForce = cv2.BFMatcher(norm)

matches = bruteForce.match(Image1_descriptors, Image2_descriptors)
```

```
matches = sorted(matches, key = lambda match:match.distance)

matched_img = cv2.drawMatches(
    Image1, Image1_key_points,
    Image2, Image2_key_points,
    matches[:100], Image2.copy())

plt.figure(figsize=(100,300))
plt.imshow(matched_img)
```

This above code applies the entire SIFT algorithm to a pair of images. But, the algorithm is saved in a Python file named `Sift_Operations.py` in the same directory as this code. Let's look at the code inside that as well.

```
import cv2
import numpy as np
import matplotlib.pyplot as plt

def extract_sift_features(img):
    sift_initialize = cv2.xfeatures2d.SIFT_create()
    key_points, descriptors = sift_initialize.
    detectAndCompute(img, None)
    return key_points, descriptors

def showing_sift_features(img1, img2, key_points):
    return plt.imshow(cv2.drawKeypoints(img1, key_points,
    img2.copy()))
```

Now let's examine the code, jumping from one file to the other as necessary:

1. In the main code, we import the important libraries: OpenCV, Numpy, Matplotlib, and the custom module `Sift_Operations. import` * means import everything that is present inside the Python file.

2. Next we read two images, to which we have to apply SIFT operations. Figure 5-1 shows the images I imported.

***Figure 5-1.** Original images*

3. Next, we convert the image to grayscale. SIFT needs gray images to perform its operations. We use the OpenCV function `cv2.cvtColor` for color format conversion.

```
Image1_gray = cv2.cvtColor(Image1, cv2.COLOR_BGR2GRAY)

Image2_gray = cv2.cvtColor(Image2, cv2.COLOR_BGR2GRAY)
```

4. Now we pass these two images to the function `extract_sift_features`, which is stored in the file `Sift_Operations.py`. This function returns the key points found in the image, and the features of those points with the name of the descriptors. Let's look at this function from the inside:

```
sift_initialize = cv2.xfeatures2d.SIFT_create()
```

   a. The previous line of code stores the entire SIFT inside the variable `sift_initialize`.

b. The `detectAndCompute` method is used to apply the algorithm to the images, w returns key points and descriptors:

```
key_points, descriptors = sift_initialize.detectAndCompute(img,
None)
```

c. The values are then returned:

```
return key_points, descriptors
```

d. Back in the calling code, these values are stored in different variables specific to the images:

```
Image1_key_points, Image1_descriptors = extract_sift_
features(Image1_gray)

Image2_key_points, Image2_descriptors = extract_sift_
features(Image2_gray)
```

5. The features are then shown so that we can look at the key points and the similarities. The method `showing_sift_features` is used to do this.

6. Let's look at this method from inside. `cv2.drawKeypoints` is used to draw the key points found in the two images.

7. The variable `norm` is then initialized and used for finding the distance between the key points. `cv2.Norm_L2` is used to calculate the Manhattan distance (Figure 5-2), which is the distance between two points measured along axes at right angles—90 degrees. It's not a straight-line distance; it follows a grid approach.

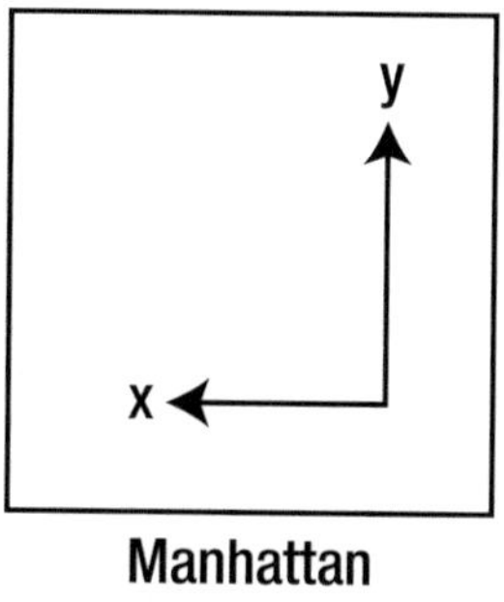

Figure 5-2. *The Manhattan distance*

8. Next, the `cv2.BFMatcher` function is initialized. It is used to find the match between descriptors of the key points. Then the `norm` variable is passed as an argument. It tells `BFMatcher` to use the Manhattan distance to perform matching. The initialized algorithm is saved in a variable called `bruteForce`.

9. The two descriptors are matched `bruteForce.match`, and then the matches are sorted based on the Manhattan distance:

```
matches = bruteForce.match(Image1_descriptors, Image2_descriptors)

matches = sorted(matches, key = lambda match:match.distance)
```

10. The key points of the two images are connected based on the top 100 sorted matches:

```
matched_img = cv2.drawMatches(

Image1, Image1_key_points,

Image2, Image2_key_points,

matches[:100], Image2.copy())
```

11. Last, the matched images are shown:

```
plt.figure(figsize=(100,300))

plt.imshow(matched_img)
```

The output of the entire code is given in Figure 5-3.

Figure 5-3. *Similarities found using the SIFT algorithm*

Image Registration Using the RANSAC Algorithm

Suppose we have two images of a single place from an aerial view. One image depicts the place using satellites whereas the second one shows a part of the same image using drones. Satellite images get updated in terms of years, whereas drone images are taken much more frequently. So, there may be a situation in which the drone image captures developments not see in the satellite image. In this scenario, we may want to put the drone image in exactly the same place where it belongs in the satellite image, but also show the latest updates. This process of putting one image over the other, at exactly the same place where it is present, is called *image registration*.

RANSAC is one of the best algorithms to use for image registration, which consists of four steps:

1. Feature detection and extraction
2. Feature matching
3. Transformation function fitting
4. Image transformation and image resampling

The RANSAC algorithm is used in the third step to find the transformation function. We take two images and then, using the RANSAC algorithm, we find the homography (similarity) between those images. Let's look at the algorithm in brief:

1. Find four common feature points of the two images randomly, then find the homography matrix*.
2. Repeat this step multiple times until we have a homography matrix with the maximum number of inliers

Let's apply this algorithm using Python. The code consists of three custom modules: `Ransac.py`, `Affine.py`, and `Align.py`. `ransac` contains the entire RANSAC algorithm, `Affine` is used for applying the rotation, translation, and scaling operation to the images. `Align` is used to align the image in such a way that it is registered perfectly on the original image.

Let's look at the code line by line:

1. First, we import the important libraries as well as the custom modules just mentioned.

```
import numpy as np
Import cv2
from Ransac import *
from Affine import *
from Align import *
```

2. Then we upload the image we want to register over the second image (the target image). Next we upload the target image.

```
img_source = cv2.imread("source.jpg")
img_target = cv2.imread("target.jpg")
```

3. Now, we use the function `extract_SIFT`, stored in the `Align` module to extract the key points and related descriptors (I explained this code in the previous section).

```
keypoint_source, descriptor_source = extract_SIFT(img_source)
keypoint_target, descriptor_target = extract_SIFT(img_target)
```

4. Next, we use the function `match_SIFT` to obtain the position of all the points found in the previous step:

```
pos = match_SIFT(descriptor_source, descriptor_target)
```

5. Inside the `match_SIFT` method, we try to obtain the best two matches, among all the matched descriptors. To do this, we use the functions `BFMatcher` and `knnMatch`. Let's look at this code snippet, saved inside the `Align` module:

```
bf = cv2.BFMatcher()
matches = bf.knnMatch(descriptor_source, descriptor_target, k=2)
```

6. We have to create an empty numpy array to store the positions of the key points. Let's name it `pos`. We put only those points inside pos that have a ratio less than or equal to 0.8, based on the ratio test by D. Lowe (see the Important terms at the end of the chapter).

```
for i in range(matches_num):
        if matches[i][0].distance <= 0.8 * matches[i][1].distance:
            temp = np.array([matches[i][0].queryIdx,
                             matches[i][0].trainIdx])
            pos = np.vstack((pos, temp))
```

7. `trainIdx` returns the index of the descriptor in source, whereas `queryIdx` returns the index of the descriptor in target. These are the actual positions that we stack vertically in the `pos` variable, and then return it.

```
return pos
```

8. Now that we have the position of the descriptors, we use the function `affine_matrix` in the `Align` module to get the homography matrix, which we use in image registration.

```
H = affine_matrix(keypoint_source, keypoint_target, pos)
```

9. Let's look inside the function:

    a. First, we store all the key points in the `s` and `t` variables, based on the best descriptor positions stored in the `pos` variable.

```
s = s[:, pos[:, 0]]
t = t[:, pos[:, 1]]
```

    b. Then we need to find the inliers. Inliers are the points in the two images that show maximum similarity, and hence can be used to draw RANSAC models. We use the function `ransac_fit`, stored in `ransac` module to get these key points.

```
_, _, inliers = ransac_fit(s, t)
```

Inside ransac_fit, we initialize a few basic variables: the number of inliers, the matrices required to do affine transformation, and a variable that stores the position of the inliers:

```
inliers_num = 0
A = None
t = None
inliers = None
```

Next, we need to find temporary matrices that help us do affine transformation. For this, we generate indices randomly for our points, then extract points from those indices to pass as a parameter to the function estimate_affine.

```
idx = np.random.randint(0, pts_s.shape[1], (K, 1))
A_tmp, t_tmp = estimate_affine(pts_s[:, idx], pts_t[:, idx])
```

Now that we have these temporary matrices, we pass them to the function residual_lengths, which calculates the error, which helps us decide the final matrix.

```
residual = residual_lengths(A_tmp, t_tmp, pts_s, pts_t)
```

An explanation of the functions residual_lengths and estimate_affine is give in the following sections. Now that we know the residual/error, we check it with the threshold. We have assigned a threshold limit of one. If the residual is less than the threshold, then we count the number of those instances.

```
inliers_tmp = np.where(residual < threshold)
```

We then compare the inliers having residual with total inliers defined (which is zero). If the residual inliers are greater than the predefined inliers, we update the predefined inlier with the new inlier value and then update the affine transformation matrices with the temporary matrices A and t. Also, we store the indices of those inliers.

```
inliers_tmp = np.where(residual < threshold)
inliers_num_tmp = len(inliers_tmp[0])
if inliers_num_tmp > inliers_num:
            inliers_num = inliers_num_tmp
            inliers = inliers_tmp
            A = A_tmp
            t = t_tmp
```

We repeat this process 2,000 times to get the best possible matrices, then return them.

```
for i in range(ITER_NUM=2000)r
return A, t, inliers
```

c. Now that we have the inlier numbers, we use them to extract the best source key points and target key points.

```
s = s[:, inliers[0]]
t = t[:, inliers[0]]
```

d. We use these key points and send them to the `estimate_affine` function, which gives us our final transformation matrices.

```
A, t = estimate_affine(s, t)
```

e. Finally, we stack the matrices horizontally and return it as one matrix: the homography matrix.

```
M = np.hstack((A, t))
return M
```

10. Now that we have our homography matrix, all that is left to do is image registration. For this, we first extract the number of rows and columns from the target image:

```
rows, cols, _ = img_target.shape
```

11. Then, will use our source image, apply the homography matrix, and scale it to the row and height of the target image:

```
warp = cv2.warpAffine(img_source, H, (cols, rows))
```

12. Now all we blend the two images. For this we give a 50% weight to the target image and a 50% weight to the warped image (The image over which we are blending the second one):

```
merge = np.uint8(img_target * 0.5 + warp * 0.5)
```

13. Now, all we have to do is show the registration. We can also save the image, based on our requirements.

```
cv2.imshow('img', merge)
cv2.waitKey(0)
cv2.destroyAllWindows()
```

estimate_affine

The `estimate_affine` function takes the total number of key points of both the source image and the target image as an input, and returns the affine transformation matrices as an output. Based on the dimension of the source key points, we initialize a dummy matrix, then fill it with source key points to be used as a loop. Then we take the target key points, reshape the dimension to 2,000 × 1, after finding its transpose. Finally, we do a linear regression on both these matrices, and get the slope and intercept of the line. Using these, we calculate the final matrices X and Y. Here is the code:

```
def estimate_affine (s, t):
    num = s.shape[1]
    M = np.zeros((2 * num, 6))

    for i in range(num):
        temp = [[s[0, i], s[1, i], 0, 0, 1, 0],
                [0, 0, s[0, i], s[1, i], 0, 1]]
        M[2 * i: 2 * i + 2, :] = np.array(temp)
    b = t.T.reshape((2 * num, 1))
    theta = np.linalg.lstsq(M, b)[0]
    X = theta[:4].reshape((2, 2))
    Y = theta[4:]
    return X, Y
```

residual_lengths

The `residual_lengths` function is used to determine the errors present in our model and to make sure the affine matrices that we generate, or the descriptors that we match, have as few errors as possible. First, we make a linear model between the affine matrices and source key points, which gives us the estimated points for the target image. We compare them with the actual target points to determine the final errors. We then subtract the target points with these estimated points, take the square of them, then find the square root to remove the effect of the negative values. This is root mean square error estimation, or residuals estimation. Last, we return the value. The code of this operation is as follows:

```
def residual_lengths(X, Y, s, t):
    e = np.dot(X, s) + Y
    diff_square = np.power(e - t, 2)
    residual = np.sqrt(np.sum(diff_square, axis=0))
    return residual
```

Processing the Images

Let's look at our target image (Figure 5-4):

Figure 5-4. *Target image*

The Complete Code

Here is the complete code for image registration:

Main Code:

```
import numpy as np
import cv2
from Ransac import *
```

```
from Affine import *
from Align import *

img_source = cv2.imread("2.jpg")
img_target = cv2.imread("target.jpg")
keypoint_source, descriptor_source = extract_SIFT(img_source)
keypoint_target, descriptor_target = extract_SIFT(img_target)
pos = match_SIFT(descriptor_source, descriptor_target)
H = affine_matrix(keypoint_source, keypoint_target, pos)

rows, cols, _ = img_target.shape
warp = cv2.warpAffine(img_source, H, (cols, rows))
merge = np.uint8(img_target * 0.5 + warp * 0.5)
cv2.imshow('img', merge)
cv2.waitKey(0)
cv2.destroyAllWindows()
```

Ransac.py:

```
import numpy as np
from Affine import *
K=3
threshold=1
ITER_NUM = 2000
def residual_lengths(X, Y, s, t):
    e = np.dot(X, s) + Y
    diff_square = np.power(e - t, 2)
    residual = np.sqrt(np.sum(diff_square, axis=0))
    return residual
def ransac_fit(pts_s, pts_t):
    inliers_num = 0
    A = None
    t = None
```

```
    inliers = None
    for i in range(ITER_NUM):
        idx = np.random.randint(0, pts_s.shape[1], (K, 1))
        A_tmp, t_tmp = estimate_affine(pts_s[:, idx], pts_t[:, idx])
        residual = residual_lengths(A_tmp, t_tmp, pts_s, pts_t)
        if not(residual is None):
            inliers_tmp = np.where(residual < threshold)
            inliers_num_tmp = len(inliers_tmp[0])
            if inliers_num_tmp > inliers_num:
                inliers_num = inliers_num_tmp
                inliers = inliers_tmp
                A = A_tmp
                t = t_tmp
        else:
            pass
    return A, t, inliers
```

Affine.py:

```
import numpy as np

def estimate_affine(s, t):
    num = s.shape[1]
    M = np.zeros((2 * num, 6))

    for i in range(num):
        temp = [[s[0, i], s[1, i], 0, 0, 1, 0],
                [0, 0, s[0, i], s[1, i], 0, 1]]
        M[2 * i: 2 * i + 2, :] = np.array(temp)
    b = t.T.reshape((2 * num, 1))
    theta = np.linalg.lstsq(M, b)[0]
    X = theta[:4].reshape((2, 2))
    Y = theta[4:]
    return X, Y
```

Align.py:

```
import numpy as np
from Ransac import *
import cv2
from Affine import *

def extract_SIFT(img):
    img_gray = cv2.cvtColor(img, cv2.COLOR_BGR2GRAY)
    sift = cv2.xfeatures2d.SIFT_create()
    kp, desc = sift.detectAndCompute(img_gray, None)
    kp = np.array([p.pt for p in kp]).T
    return kp, desc
def match_SIFT(descriptor_source, descriptor_target):
    bf = cv2.BFMatcher()
    matches = bf.knnMatch(descriptor_source, descriptor_target,
    k=2)
    pos = np.array([], dtype=np.int32).reshape((0, 2))
    matches_num = len(matches)
    for i in range(matches_num):
        if matches[i][0].distance <= 0.8 * matches[i][1].distance:
            temp = np.array([matches[i][0].queryIdx,
                             matches[i][0].trainIdx])
            pos = np.vstack((pos, temp))
    return pos

def affine_matrix(s, t, pos):
    s = s[:, pos[:, 0]]
    t = t[:, pos[:, 1]]
    _, _, inliers = ransac_fit(s, t)
    s = s[:, inliers[0]]
    t = t[:, inliers[0]]
```

```
    A, t = estimate_affine(s, t)
    M = np.hstack((A, t))
    return M
```

Image Classification Using Artificial Neural Networks

Before applying artificial neural networks over a set of images for classification, let's first examine what neural networks are. For example, what happens when we get hurt? A signal is sent immediately to our brain, and then the brain responds based on the intensity of the signal. The transfer of the signal takes place via neurons. The neurons transfer the signal, in the form of a synapse, to another neuron, and the process continues until the signal reaches the brain. The structure of a neuron is presented in Figure 5-5.

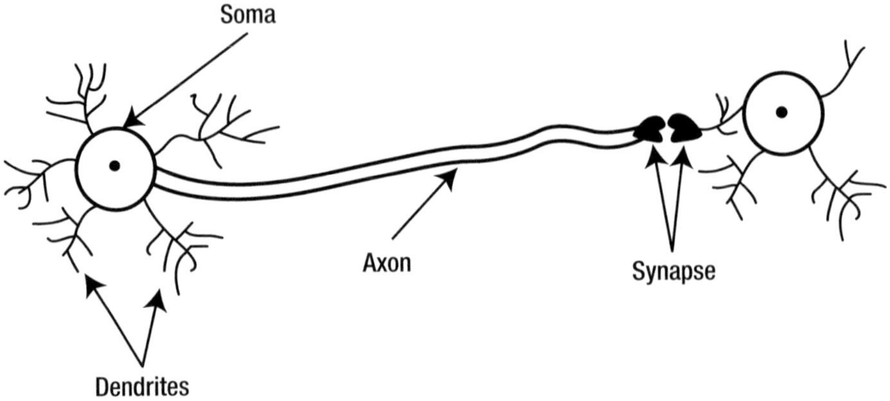

Figure 5-5. *Biological neuron*

The information in Figure 5-5 that is important to us includes the dendrites and the axon. The dendrites receive the signal from another neuron, and the axon transmits the signal to the next neuron. This chain stops at the last node, which is brain.

Artificial neural networks use the same analogy, and process information using artificial neurons. Information is transferred from one artificial neuron to another, which finally leads to an activation function, which acts like a brain and makes a decision. The structure of a simple artificial neural network is shown in Figure 5-6.

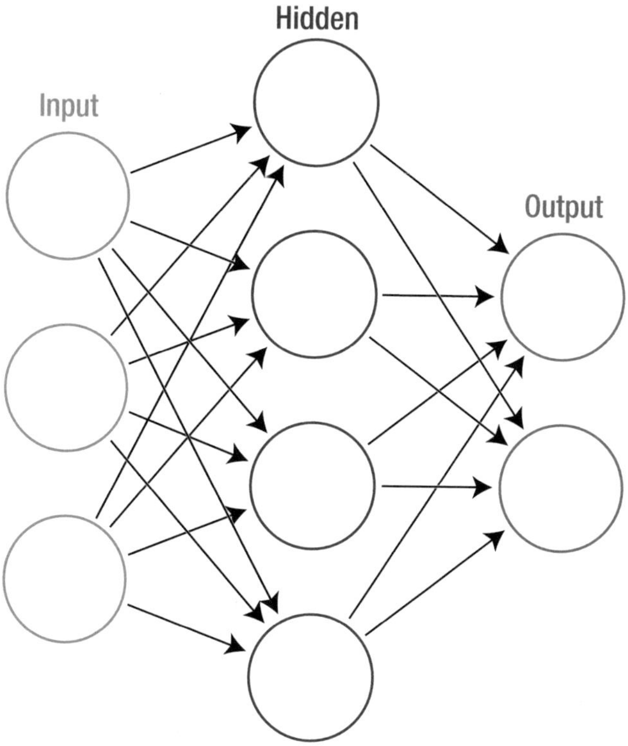

***Figure 5-6.** Simple artificial neural network*

So the information to be processed is stored in input nodes. Next come the hidden layers, where the information is actually processed. Last, there is the output . The activation function is between the hidden layer and the output layer. We call the layer *hidden* because we cannot see what happens inside the hidden layer. There can be one or more hidden layers in the artificial neural network architecture. The greater the number of hidden layers, the deeper the network (versus a shallow network).

Now if we delve into the complete details of neural networks, this book will become very long, and we'll digress from our main topic: image processing. Therefore, instead of going into neural networks in detail, I advise you to study them on your own. That said, now let's move on to the application of artificial neural networks for handwriting recognition. I highly recommend that you do not proceed further without having a good knowledge base of neural networks.

The Modified National Institute of Standards and Technology (MNIST) database includes a dataset that contains approximately 60,000 training images and 10,000 testing images of handwritten digits. We'll use the training dataset* to train our neural network, and then we'll use the test dataset* to look at its accuracy. Finally, you can give your own handwritten digit to check the predictions by our trained model.

First, let us look at a flowchart of how to proceed with neural networks (Figure 5-7).

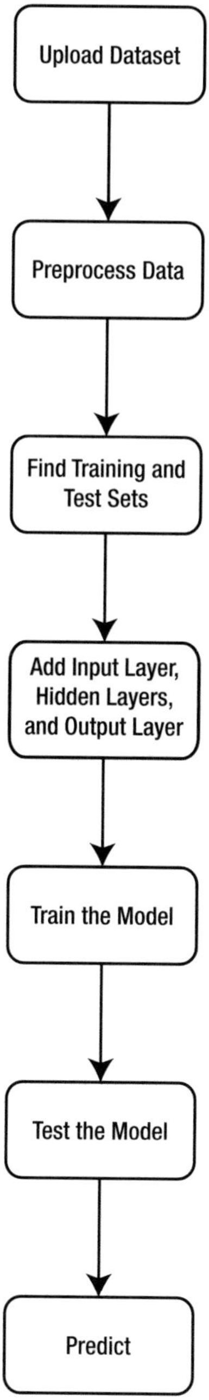

Figure 5-7. *Process flowchart*

First, we have to download the train and test datasets from the MNIST database. We can download them from the kaggle web site (`https://www.kaggle.com/c/digit-recognizer/data#`).

After the data are downloaded, we need to upload the data to our Python environment.

```
import pandas as pd
input_data = pd.read_csv("train.csv")
```

Now let's look at our training set. It consists of 785 columns. Each image has 28 × 28 resolution. Therefore, 784 columns contain the pixel values of each digit. The last indicates the actual number represented by the pixel values. Let's look at the preview of the images and the dataset (Figure 5-8).

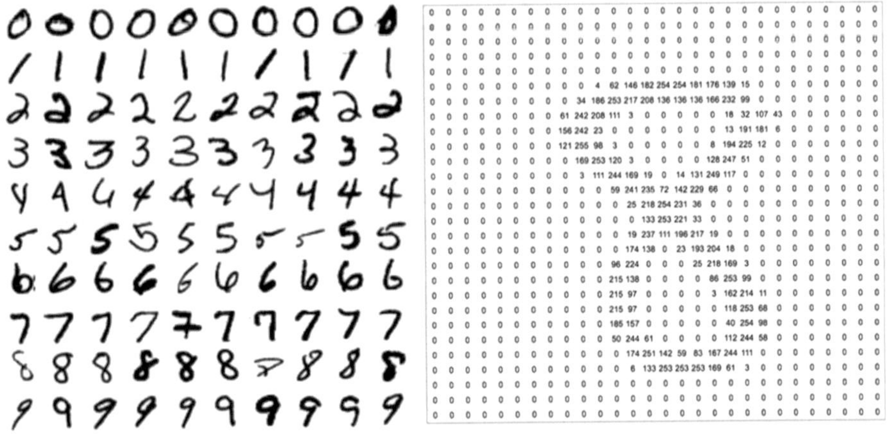

Figure 5-8. *MNIST dataset*

We must create two data frames in Python. One will store all the pixel values X; the other will store the actual number y.

```
y = input_data['label']
input_data.drop('label', axis=1, inplace = True)
X = input_data
```

Now we convert the labels present in y into dummies (see Important terms).

```
y = pd.get_dummies(y)
```

Now that we have our data in X and y, we can start with our neural network. Let's create four hidden layers, one input layer, and one output layer using Keras.

```
classifier = Sequential()
classifier.add(Dense(units = 600, kernel_initializer =
'uniform', activation = 'relu', input_dim = 784))
classifier.add(Dense(units = 400, kernel_initializer =
'uniform', activation = 'relu'))
classifier.add(Dense(units = 200, kernel_initializer =
'uniform', activation = 'relu'))
classifier.add(Dense(units = 10, kernel_initializer =
'uniform', activation = 'sigmoid'))
```

The first hidden layer has 600 neurons, the second has 400, the third has 200, and the last has ten neurons. We then initialize the parameters `w` and `b` in normalized format by giving `kernel_initializer = 'uniform'`. In the first three layers, we give activation function `relu`; the last layer contains the `sigmoid` function. Also, the first layer contains the input dimension of 784. Our network now looks like that depicted in Figure 5-9.

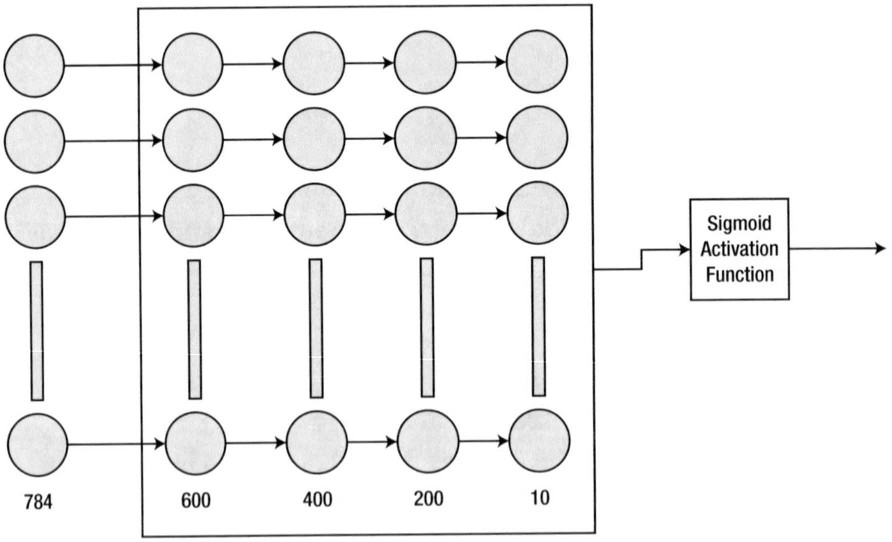

Figure 5-9. *Deep neural network*

Note In Figure 5-9, each and every node is connected to each and every node of the next layer.

Now we need to compute the stochastic gradient descent algorithm* to minimize the loss:

```
classifier.compile(optimizer = 'sgd', loss = 'mean_squared_
error', metrics = ['accuracy'])
```

Finally, we start the training by giving a batch size* of ten and epochs* of ten:

```
classifier.fit(X_train, y_train, batch_size = 10, epochs = 10)
```

This gives us an accuracy of 98.95. Let's look at the output:

```
Epoch 1/10
42000/42000 [==============================] - 55s 1ms/step - loss: 0.0207 - acc: 0.8769
Epoch 2/10
42000/42000 [==============================] - 58s 1ms/step - loss: 0.0091 - acc: 0.9505
Epoch 3/10
42000/42000 [==============================] - 57s 1ms/step - loss: 0.0067 - acc: 0.9643
Epoch 4/10
42000/42000 [==============================] - 51s 1ms/step - loss: 0.0053 - acc: 0.9713
Epoch 5/10
42000/42000 [==============================] - 52s 1ms/step - loss: 0.0043 - acc: 0.9771
Epoch 6/10
42000/42000 [==============================] - 59s 1ms/step - loss: 0.0036 - acc: 0.9806
Epoch 7/10
42000/42000 [==============================] - 59s 1ms/step - loss: 0.0031 - acc: 0.9837
Epoch 8/10
42000/42000 [==============================] - 59s 1ms/step - loss: 0.0026 - acc: 0.9857
Epoch 9/10
42000/42000 [==============================] - 59s 1ms/step - loss: 0.0023 - acc: 0.9876
Epoch 10/10
42000/42000 [==============================] - 60s 1ms/step - loss: 0.0020 - acc: 0.9895
```

Finally, we predict on the test dataset. First we upload it, then we do the predictions:

```
test_data = pd.read_csv("test.csv")
y_pred = classifier.predict(test_data)
```

All the predictions get saved inside the variable y_pred.

Let's look at the full code:

```
import pandas as pd
import keras
from keras.models import Sequential
from keras.layers import Dense

input_data = pd.read_csv("train.csv")

y = input_data['label']
input_data.drop('label',axis=1,inplace = True)
X = input_data
y = pd.get_dummies(y)

classifier = Sequential()
```

```
classifier.add(Dense(units = 600, kernel_initializer =
'uniform', activation = 'relu', input_dim = 784))
classifier.add(Dense(units = 400, kernel_initializer =
'uniform', activation = 'relu'))
classifier.add(Dense(units = 200, kernel_initializer =
'uniform', activation = 'relu'))
classifier.add(Dense(units = 10, kernel_initializer =
'uniform', activation = 'sigmoid'))
classifier.compile(optimizer = 'sgd', loss = 'mean_squared_
error', metrics = ['accuracy'])

classifier.fit(X, y, batch_size = 10, epochs = 10)

test_data = pd.read_csv("test.csv")
y_pred = classifier.predict(test_data)
```

Image Classification Using CNNs

CNNs are used for image processing and classification problems. In the previous section, we saw how to use an artificial neural network and apply it to an MNIST dataset. In this section, we have a look at CNNs and their application to the same dataset.

With CNNs, there are a few extra layers, apart from the normal neural network layers. In the previous section, we saw that each and every node is connected to each and every node of the next layer. This can become time-consuming and also leads to the problem of overfitting*. CNNs are used to rectify this issue. With CNNs, we don't have a connection to each and every node. With CNNs, we apply selective filtering. Figure 5-10 shows the basic structure of a simple CNN.

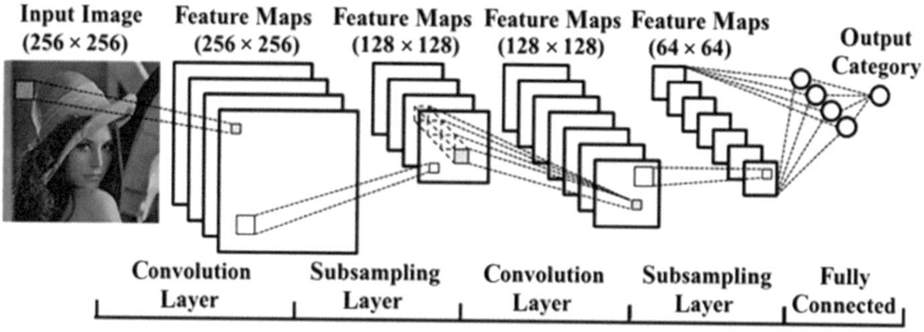

Figure 5-10. *Summary of a CNN*

A brief summary of how CNNs work starts with the convolution layer, where we apply a filter (also known as a *kernel*) to the input image. This kernel strides over the image, block by block, where each block is a collection of pixel cells. During this process, we perform matrix multiplication, which results in a lower resolution image. In the subsampling layer (also called the *downsampling layer*) we find the average pixel value (called the *average pooling*) or the maximum pixel value (called the *max pooling*), and get an even lower resolution image. Last, the output gets connected to the fully connected layer, where each max pooling output is connected to each node in the fully connected layer. After this, a neural network architecture is followed. For detailed explanation of how CNNs work, see the course by Andrew Ng on Coursera (`https://www.coursera.org/learn/neural-networks-deep-learning`).

Let's look how to apply a CNN to the MNIST dataset. First, we create a Python file with the name `load_and_preprocess` and import it into our code to do data preprocessing. Then we find the training and test datasets. In this code I do not use the test dataset provided by Kaggle; instead, I show you how to bifurcate the data into a training dataset and a test dataset, and then check the accuracy of the test dataset. First let us analyze the code of the `load_and_preprocess` module.

1. First, we define the dimension of the image. Each image in the dataset is 28 × 28. We'll save the number of pixel rows and number of pixel columns inside variables `r` and `c`:

```
r, c = 28, 28
```

2. We then define the number of classes using labels of 0 to 9, which means there is a total of ten classes:

```
num_classes = 10
```

3. Inside the `keras` module, we have the entire MNIST dataset. So, instead of using the `.csv` sheet downloaded from Kaggle, we use the dataset from Keras directly:

```
from keras.datasets import mnist
```

4. Next, we extract the training and test sets out of it by calling the built-in method inside Keras called `load_data()`:

```
(x_train, y_train), (x_test, y_test) = mnist.load_data()
```

5. Then we reshape the functionality of numpy. Currently the data are in an array format with no proper structure. Using `reshape`, we give the data structure. We do this by telling Python to convert the array in such a way that it has all the pixel values in one column only:

```
x_train = x_train.reshape(x_train.shape[0], r, c, 1)
x_test = x_test.reshape(x_test.shape[0], r, c, 1)
```

6. Currently, the data type of `x_train` and `x_test` is Int (integer). We want to convert it to Float, so we can apply preprocessing over it easily:

```
x_train = x_train.astype('float32')
x_test = x_test.astype('float32')
```

7. Now we need to do normalization. We divide each and every pixel with the highest pixel intensity value of 255, so that the data result in a lower range of zero to one. This helps in training the model efficiently.

```
x_train /= 255
x_test /= 255
```

8. Now that we have taken care of the independent variables*, we need to take care of dependent variables*, which are the actual number labels. To do this, we convert the values, which are currently in integer format, to categorical values*:

```
y_train = keras.utils.to_categorical(y_train, num_classes)
y_test = keras.utils.to_categorical(y_test, num_classes)
```

9. Last, we return all the processed data back to our original code:

```
return (x_train,x_test,y_train,y_test,input_shape)
```

Let's look at the complete code:

```
from keras.datasets import mnist
import keras

def load_and_preprocess():
    r, c = 28, 28
```

```
    num_classes = 10
    x_train, y_train, x_test, y_test = mnist.load_data()
    x_train = x_train.reshape(x_train.shape[0], r, c, 1)
    x_test = x_test.reshape(x_test.shape[0], r, c, 1)
    input_shape = (r, c, 1)

    x_train = x_train.astype('float32')
    x_test = x_test.astype('float32')

    x_train /= 255
    x_test /= 255

    # convert class vectors to binary class matrices
    y_train = keras.utils.to_categorical(y_train, num_classes)
    y_test = keras.utils.to_categorical(y_test, num_classes)
    return (x_train,x_test,y_train,y_test,input_shape)
```

Coming to our main code, we will now declare our Convolution and Subsampling Layers:

```
model = Sequential()
model.add(Conv2D(32, kernel_size=(3, 3), activation='relu',
input_shape=input_shape))
model.add(Conv2D(64, (3, 3), activation='relu'))
model.add(MaxPooling2D(pool_size=(2, 2)))
model.add(Dropout(0.25))
model.add(Flatten())
model.add(Dense(128, activation='relu'))
model.add(Dropout(0.5))
model.add(Dense(num_classes, activation='softmax'))
```

In the previous code, we defined two convolution layers using the function `Conv2D`. The output of the second one is given to the subsampling layer. `Dropout` is used for making our training avoid overfitting. Its value lies between zero and one, and we can experiment with different values to find better accuracy. The Dense function helps to give the output of the relu or softmax (see Important terms) activation functions.

Next, we minimize errors by using the AdaDelta algorithm (see Important terms):

```
model.compile(loss=keras.losses.categorical_crossentropy,
optimizer=keras.optimizers.Adadelta(), metrics=['accuracy'])
```

Finally, we start the training with a batch size of 128 and epochs of 12. We give the parameter validation data, so it can apply the trained model to the test dataset and allow us to see the accuracy of that as well.

```
model.fit(x_train, y_train, batch_size=128, epochs=12,
validation_data=(x_test, y_test))
```

To print the accuracy, we use the following code:

```
score = model.evaluate(x_test, y_test, verbose=0)
print('Test loss:', score[0])
print('Test accuracy:', score[1])
```

Let's look at the full code. The output is presented in Figure 5-11.

Main Code

```
import keras
from keras.models import Sequential
from keras.layers import Dense, Dropout, Flatten
from keras.layers import Conv2D, MaxPooling2D
from Load_and_Preprocess import *

x_train,x_test,y_train,y_test, input_shape = load_and_preprocess()
num_classes=10
model = Sequential()
model.add(Conv2D(32, kernel_size=(3,
3),activation='relu',input_shape=input_shape))
model.add(Conv2D(64, (3, 3), activation='relu'))
```

```
model.add(MaxPooling2D(pool_size=(2, 2)))
model.add(Dropout(0.25))
model.add(Flatten())
model.add(Dense(128, activation='relu'))

model.add(Dropout(0.5))

model.add(Dense(num_classes, activation='softmax'))

model.compile(loss=keras.losses.categorical_crossentropy,
              optimizer=keras.optimizers.Adadelta(),
              metrics=['accuracy'])

model.fit(x_train, y_train,
          batch_size=128,
          epochs=12,
          validation_data=(x_test, y_test))

score = model.evaluate(x_test, y_test, verbose=0)
print('Test loss:', score[0])
print('Test accuracy:', score[1])
```

Load_and_Preprocess

```
from keras.datasets import mnist
import keras

def load_and_preprocess():
    r, c = 28, 28
    num_classes = 10
    (x_train, y_train), (x_test, y_test) = mnist.load_data()
    x_train = x_train.reshape(x_train.shape[0], r, c, 1)
    x_test = x_test.reshape(x_test.shape[0], r, c, 1)
    input_shape = (r, c, 1)
```

```
    x_train = x_train.astype('float32')
    x_test = x_test.astype('float32')

    x_train /= 255
    x_test /= 255
    y_train = keras.utils.to_categorical(y_train, num_classes)
    y_test = keras.utils.to_categorical(y_test, num_classes)
    return (x_train,x_test,y_train,y_test,input_shape)
```

Output

```
Train on 60000 samples, validate on 10000 samples
Epoch 1/12
60000/60000 [==============================] - 182s 3ms/step - loss: 0.2589 - acc: 0.9206 - val_loss: 0.0558 - val_acc: 0.9820
Epoch 2/12
60000/60000 [==============================] - 180s 3ms/step - loss: 0.0868 - acc: 0.9748 - val_loss: 0.0425 - val_acc: 0.9853
Epoch 3/12
60000/60000 [==============================] - 182s 3ms/step - loss: 0.0664 - acc: 0.9804 - val_loss: 0.0327 - val_acc: 0.9883
Epoch 4/12
60000/60000 [==============================] - 187s 3ms/step - loss: 0.0537 - acc: 0.9839 - val_loss: 0.0311 - val_acc: 0.9889
Epoch 5/12
60000/60000 [==============================] - 197s 3ms/step - loss: 0.0459 - acc: 0.9862 - val_loss: 0.0310 - val_acc: 0.9893
Epoch 6/12
60000/60000 [==============================] - 187s 3ms/step - loss: 0.0407 - acc: 0.9875 - val_loss: 0.0304 - val_acc: 0.9897
Epoch 7/12
60000/60000 [==============================] - 187s 3ms/step - loss: 0.0364 - acc: 0.9895 - val_loss: 0.0294 - val_acc: 0.9901
Epoch 8/12
60000/60000 [==============================] - 183s 3ms/step - loss: 0.0340 - acc: 0.9898 - val_loss: 0.0290 - val_acc: 0.9907
Epoch 9/12
60000/60000 [==============================] - 183s 3ms/step - loss: 0.0311 - acc: 0.9907 - val_loss: 0.0265 - val_acc: 0.9917
Epoch 10/12
60000/60000 [==============================] - 183s 3ms/step - loss: 0.0285 - acc: 0.9915 - val_loss: 0.0252 - val_acc: 0.9920
Epoch 11/12
60000/60000 [==============================] - 184s 3ms/step - loss: 0.0275 - acc: 0.9914 - val_loss: 0.0264 - val_acc: 0.9920
Epoch 12/12
60000/60000 [==============================] - 184s 3ms/step - loss: 0.0264 - acc: 0.9921 - val_loss: 0.0264 - val_acc: 0.9918
Test loss: 0.026368951098990512
Test accuracy: 0.9918
```

Figure 5-11. *Output of code*

Image Classification Using Machine Learning Approaches

In this section we look at the application of three famous machine learning algorithms:

- Decision trees
- Support vector machines (SVMs)
- Logistic regression

First, let's examine the basics of these three algorithms. Then we apply them to the MNIST dataset, which—as mentioned earlier—is a huge database of handwritten digits. We use this dataset for handwriting recognition.

Decision Trees

When we want to make a big decision in our lives, we do a pro and con analysis. Decision trees are similar to this method. Based on a certain statistical threshold, we determine whether a particular thing belongs to one class or the another. Suppose we want to find out whether a person is Indian or a foreigner. The first threshold could be to look at skin color. The next threshold could be voice tone. Another threshold could be physique. After applying all these thresholds, we make a tree that helps us determine the category in which that person belongs. We don't study the statistical details, but some of the important terms related to decision trees are as follows:

- *Node*: A block in the tree
- *Pure node*: A node containing single class elements, such as people who are foreigners
- *Purity*: The degree of the same class elements in one node
- *Entropy*: A statistical method used for determining a threshold
- *Information gain*: The difference between entropies of two levels of nodes; used to decide when to stop tree generation

Support Vector Machines

SVMs use the concept of mathematical planes (maximum-margin hyperplanes) to distinguish between multiple classes. So, using our previous example, SVMs draw a plane between two classes—in our case, Indians and foreigners. We try to maximize the distance of this plane from both classes, which is why it's called the *maximum-margin hyperplane*. To construct this hyperplane, we use the concept of support vectors, which are the outermost points of each class. In case of linear classification (see Important terms), this margin is drawn directly. But, when it comes to nonlinear classifications, SVMs use the kernel trick to convert nonlinear to linear, and then find the hyperplane.

Logistic Regression

Logistic regression is one of the most famous algorithms in machine learning. It is a modified form of linear regression in which we use logits to determine the probability of an element belonging to a particular class. It gives us an output between zero and one. If the output is greater than 0.5, the element is said to belong to one class; otherwise, it belongs to the other. We can also draw a curve to test the efficiency of our model.

Code

Now that we know the basics of all three algorithms, let's apply them to our dataset. The first step is to read the dataset using the pandas library and store it in the variable `data`:

```
import pandas as pd
data = pd.read_csv("train.csv")
```

Next, we find our dependent and independent variables. We store our dependent variable in variable y and our independent variable in X:

```
y = data['label']
data.drop('label',axis=1,inplace = True)
X = data
y = pd.Categorical(y)
```

After we do this, we import our three algorithms, which are saved in the sklearn module:

```
from sklearn.linear_model import LogisticRegression
from sklearn.tree import DecisionTreeClassifier
from sklearn.svm import LinearSVC
```

With the libraries imported, we have to make an instance of them:

```
logreg = LogisticRegression()
dt = DecisionTreeClassifier()
svc = LinearSVC()
```

Now our entire algorithm is stored in three respective variables: logreg, dt, and svc. Next, we have to train our model. We call the fit function, which starts the training directly:

```
model_logreg = logreg.fit(X,y)
model_dt = dt.fit(X,y)
model_svc = svc.fit(X,y)
```

After we have our trained models saved in our variables, we try to predict the new values present in the test dataset:

```
X_test = pd.read_csv("test.csv")
pred_logreg = model_logreg.predict(X_test)
pred_dt = model_logreg.predict(X_test)
pred_svc = model_logreg.predict(X_test)
```

We can also check the accuracy of our trained model on the train dataset:

```
from sklearn.accuracy import accuracy_score
pred1 = model_logreg.predict(X)
pred2 = model_dt.predict(X)
pred3 = model_svc.predict(X)
print("Decision Tree Accuracy is: ", accuracy_score(pred1, y)*100)
print("Logistic Regression Accuracy is: ", accuracy_
score(pred2, y)*100)
print("Support Vector Machine Accuracy is: ", accuracy_
score(pred3, y)*100)
```

Let's look at the complete code and output:

```
import pandas as pd
data = pd.read_csv("train.csv")
y = data['label']
data.drop('label',axis=1,inplace = True)
X = data
y = pd.Categorical(y)
from sklearn.linear_model import LogisticRegression
from sklearn.tree import DecisionTreeClassifier
from sklearn.svm import LinearSVC
logreg = LogisticRegression()
dt = DecisionTreeClassifier()
svc = LinearSVC()
model_logreg = logreg.fit(X,y)
model_dt = dt.fit(X,y)
model_svc = svc.fit(X,y)
X_test = pd.read_csv("test.csv")
pred_logreg = model_logreg.predict(X_test)
pred_dt = model_dt.predict(X_test)
pred_svc = model_svc.predict(X_test)
```

```
from sklearn.accuracy import accuracy_score
pred1 = model_logreg.predict(X)
pred2 = model_dt.predict(X)
pred3 = model_svc.predict(X)
print("Decision Tree Accuracy is: ", accuracy_score(pred_dt,
y)*100)
print("Logistic Regression Accuracy is: ", accuracy_score(pred_
logreg, y)*100)
print("Support Vector Machine Accuracy is: ", accuracy_
score(pred_svc, y)*100)
```

```
Output:
```

```
Decision Tree Accuracy is: 100.0
Logistic Regression Accuracy is: 93.8547619047619
Support Vector Machine Accuracy is: 88.26190476190476
```

Important Terms

AdaDelta algorithm an alternative to the gradient descent algorithm; the model learns from the dataset automatically without predefining the learning rate (mandatory in the gradient descent algorithm); helps to eliminate the problems of overfitting and underfitting

batch size parts of data (batches) passed one at a time inside a model until the dataset is over; after all the batches are processed, the result is one epoch

categorical values labels that are not numerical (e.g., cats, dogs, high, medium, low); opposite of use in the MNIST dataset, where labels are numbers, which makes predictions more effective

dependent variable an element we are actually predicting

dummies when we convert categorical variables to binary numbers assigned to each category

epochs the number of steps a model takes to minimize error

gradient descent algorithm used to minimize error based on the concepts of backpropagation and differentiation; the model learns from this algorithm all the important features present in the dataset, which helps it make efficient predictions

homography matrix a way of mapping two images to find the common patterns between them; used for image registration

independent variable element used to predict dependent variables

linear classification a way of classifying elements based on straight-line bifurcation

overfitting when a model takes into consideration all features, including unnecessary features; gives the wrong results

ratio test by Dr. Lowe a test used to determine whether the features extracted from the images can be used to find the similarity between them

`softmax` an activation function used for making classifications after a model is done with the training; helps to decide in which category the element belong; has a value between zero and one

test set part of a dataset in which we test the efficiency of our model

training set part of a dataset used to train and make a model

underfitting when a model is unable to take care of all the important features present, and thus gives wrong results

CHAPTER 6

Real-time Use Cases

Now that we have looked at the basics and advanced concepts of image processing, it's time to look at some real-time use cases. In this chapter we look at five different POCs, which can be tweaked based on your own requirements:

1. Finding Palm Lines
2. Detecting Faces
3. Recognizing Faces
4. Tracking Movements
5. Detecting Lanes

Finding Palm Lines

We will use Python and the OpenCV library to determine the major palm lines present in our palm. First, we need to read the original image:

```
import cv2
image = cv2.imread("palm.jpg")
cv2.imshow("palm",image) #to view the palm in python
cv2.waitKey(0)
```

Now we convert the image to grayscale:

```
gray = cv2.cvtColor(image,cv2.COLOR_BGR2GRAY)
```


H. Singh, *Practical Machine Learning and Image Processing*,
https://doi.org/10.1007/978-1-4842-4149-3_6

Then we use the filter algorithm Canny Edge Detector to find the palm lines. For different images, we need to change the parameters accordingly.

```
edges = cv2.Canny(gray,40,55,apertureSize = 3)
cv2.imshow("edges in palm",edges)
cv2.waitKey(0)
```

Now we revert the colors so that recognized lines are to black:

```
edges = cv2.bitwise_not(edges)
```

Output:

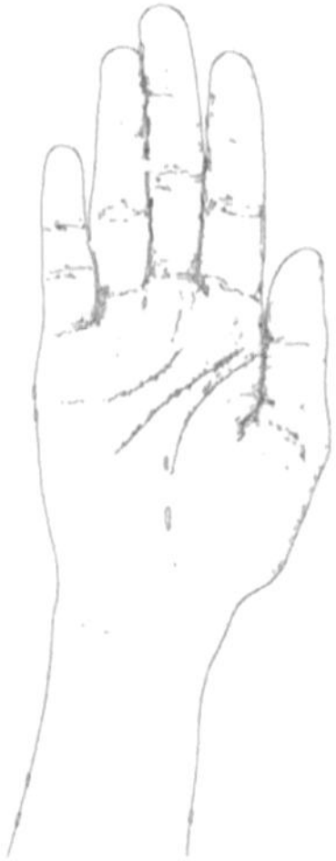

Next, we blend the previous image, with the original image:

```
cv2.imwrite("palmlines.jpg", edges)
palmlines = cv2.imread("palmlines.jpg")
img = cv2.addWeighted(palmlines, 0.3, image, 0.7, 0)
```

```
Final Output:
```

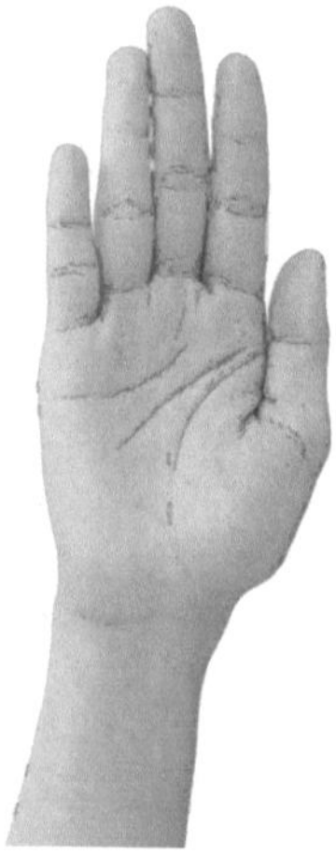

We can change the parameters to get more effective output.

Detecting Faces

In this section we apply facial recognition code to an image containing a face, then apply the same code to an image with multiple faces. The first thing we must do is import the important libraries:

```
import cv2
import matplotlib.pyplot as plt
```

Next we read the image containing one face. After reading it, we convert it to grayscale, then show it in a new window:

```
img1 = cv2.imread("single_face.jpg")
gray_img = cv2.cvtColor(img11, cv2.COLOR_BGR2GRAY)
cv2.imshow("Original_grayscale_image",gray_img)
cv2.waitKey(0)
```

Now we need to apply Haar Cascade over the image. We have several Haar Cascades to detect multiple things already stored in the OpenCV project. For convenience, I've attached the required cascades, stored in the XML file format, in the sharepoint of this book. The following is a list of cascades:

- haarcascade_eye.xml
- haarcascade_eye_tree_eyeglasses.xml
- haarcascade_frontalcatface.xml
- haarcascade_frontalface_alt.xml
- haarcascade_frontalface_alt2.xml
- haarcascade_frontalface_alt_tree.xml
- haarcascade_frontalface_default.xml
- haarcascade_fullbody.xml
- haarcascade_lefteye_2splits.xml
- haarcascade_lowerbody.xml
- haarcascade_profileface.xml
- haarcascade_righteye_2splits.xml
- haarcascade_smile.xml
- haarcascade_upperbody.xml

In our case, we'll use haarcascade_frontalface_alt.xml:

```
haar_face_cascade = cv2.CascadeClassifier('haarcascade_
frontalface_alt.xml')
faces = haar_face_cascade.detectMultiScale(gray_img,
scaleFactor=1.1, minNeighbors=5)
for (x, y, w, h) in faces:
    cv2.rectangle(img1, (x, y), (x+w, y+h), (0, 255, 0), 2)
```

The previous code loads the cascading algorithm in a variable. Then, using that algorithm, it tries to detect the faces and draw a circle over the detected face. `scaleFactor` is used to take care of large and small faces. If you are closer to the camera, you appear to have a large face; otherwise, it appears smaller. `minNeighbors` looks at the face detected inside a rectangle and decides what to include and what to reject. Now, let's show the detected image:

```
cv2.imshow("Final_detected_image",cv2.COLOR_BGR2RGB(img1))
cv2.waitKey(0)
```

The previous lines of code give the following output:

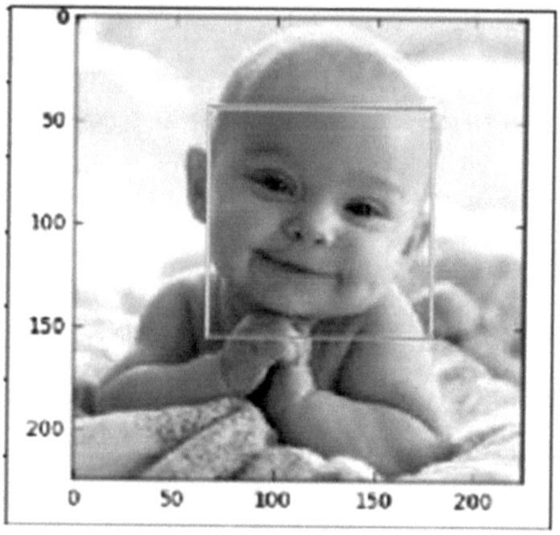

If, we use another image containing multiple faces, instead of one face, the code gives this output:

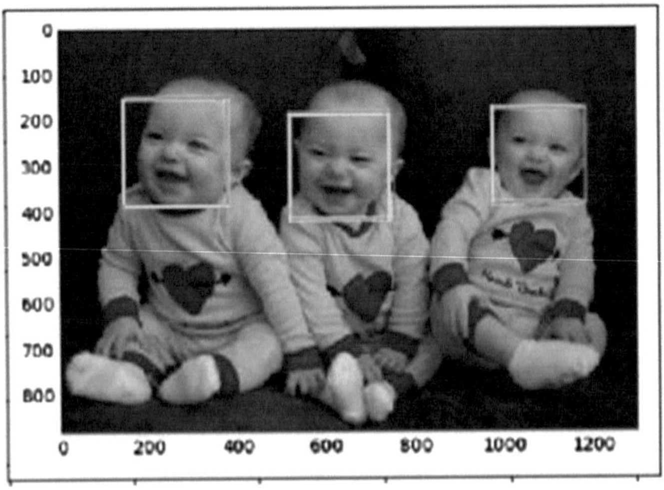

Recognizing Faces

We have successfully detected the faces present in the image, but how do we recognize which face belongs to whom? To figure this out, we will use advanced OpenCV methods.

The first step is to detect the face. We incorporate exactly the same code from the previous section inside the method detect_face():

```
def detect_face(img):
    gray = cv2.cvtColor(img, cv2.COLOR_BGR2GRAY)
    face_cascade = cv2.CascadeClassifier('haarcascade_
    frontalface_alt.xml')
    faces = face_cascade.detectMultiScale(gray,
    scaleFactor=1.2, minNeighbors=5)
    (x, y, w, h) = faces[0]
    return gray[y:y+w, x:x+h], faces[0]
```

Instead of drawing a rectangle around the face, the code returns the coordinates.

The next step is to provide sufficient data so the system can learn that multiple faces belong to a specific person. Next time, it will be able to identify the person from a new image.

```
def prepare_training_data(data_folder_path):
    dirs = os.listdir(data_folder_path)
    faces = []
    labels = []
    for dir_name in dirs:
        if not dir_name.startswith("s"):
            continue
        label = int(dir_name.replace("s", ""))
        subject_dir_path = data_folder_path + "/" + dir_name
        subject_images_names = os.listdir(subject_dir_path)
        for image_name in subject_images_names:
            image_path = subject_dir_path + "/" + image_name
            image = cv2.imread(image_path)
            face, rect = detect_face(image)
            if face is not None:
                faces.append(face)
                labels.append(label)
    cv2.waitKey(0)
    cv2.destroyAllWindows()
    return faces, labels
```

The previous code first reads each and every image present inside a specific folder, then tries to detect the face and store the face coordinates in lists `faces[]` and `labels[]`. In this code, the name of the person should be the folder name, and all the images of that person should be kept in the folder. The above function returns all the face coordinates and labels, which later help to train the data.

Next comes the training part. For this, we'll use LBPHFaceRecognizer function. Let's apply the training function to the faces and labels:

```
face_recognizer = cv2.face.LBPHFaceRecognizer_create()
face_recognizer.train(faces, np.array(labels))
```

This code trains the model, looking at the face coordinates and the labels.

The next thing we need to do is predict. Suppose we try to recognize two faces. I've taken Ranveer and Sachin Tendulkar's images. The model has been trained on these images, and it will try to predict new images.

```
subjects = ["", "Sachin Tendulkar", "Ranveer"]
img = "ranveer.jpg"
face, rect = detect_face(img)
label= face_recognizer.predict(face)[0]
label_text = subjects[label]
(x, y, w, h) = rect
cv2.rectangle(img, (x, y), (x+w, y+h), (0, 255, 0), 2)
cv2.putText(img, label_text, (rect[0], rect[1]-5), cv2.FONT_
HERSHEY_PLAIN, 1.5, (0, 255, 0), 2)
```

This code reads the image and tries to predict whether the image is of Ranveer. Let's see the output of this code. The entire code is present in the sharepoint.

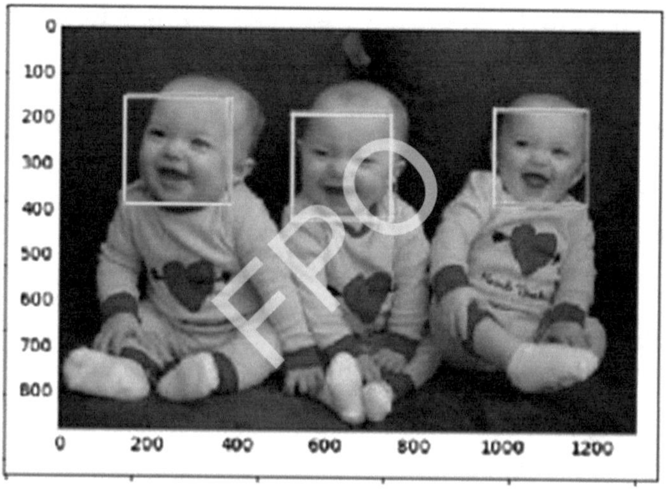

Tracking Movements

Suppose you have a pen, but instead of writing on a piece of paper, you write in the air and things get written automatically. Sound like magic? Well, it's possible to do this using advanced image processing methods.

Suppose I have a maker with a blue nib. I want to move it in the air and have a camera track the blue nib and draw exactly the same movements on the screen. Let's see how we can make this happen.

First, we have to capture only the blue nib. This means that all the other things—the hand, the background, and so on—are nothing but noise. We have to remove the noise, and we do so using erosion and dilation for. Let's look at the code:

```
mask=cv2.inRange(hsv,Lower_green,Upper_green)
mask = cv2.erode(mask, kernel, iterations=2)
mask=cv2.morphologyEx(mask,cv2.MORPH_OPEN,kernel)
mask = cv2.dilate(mask, kernel, iterations=1)
res=cv2.bitwise_and(img,img,mask=mask)
cnts,heir=cv2.findContours(mask.copy(),cv2.RETR_EXTERNAL,cv2.
CHAIN_APPROX_SIMPLE)[-2:]
```

Next, we have to define the range of blue colors that we want:

```
Lower_green = np.array([110,50,50])
Upper_green = np.array([130,255,255])
```

Now we need to track the movement. To do this, we find the contours, and then the moments, of the image, which are used later to draw the lines. To learn more about image moments and contours, refer to the Appendix.

```
if len(cnts) > 0:
        c = max(cnts, key=cv2.contourArea)
        ((x, y), radius) = cv2.minEnclosingCircle©
        M = cv2.moments©
        center = (int(M["m10"] / M["m00"]), int(M["m01"] /
        M["m00"]))
        if radius > 5:
            cv2.circle(img, (int(x), int(y)), int(radius),(0,
            255, 255), 2)
            cv2.circle(img, center, 5, (0,0,255), -1)
    pts.appendleft(center)
    for i in range(1,len(pts)):
        if pts[i-1]is None or pts[i] is None:
            continue
        thick = int(np.sqrt(len(pts) / float(i + 1)) * 2.5)
        cv2.line(img, pts[i-1],pts[i],(0,0,248),thick)
```

Finally, our code is ready. Let's see whether our code tracks the pen.

```
cv2.imshow("Frame", img)
cv2.imshow("mask",mask)
cv2.imshow("res",res)
```

We get the following output:

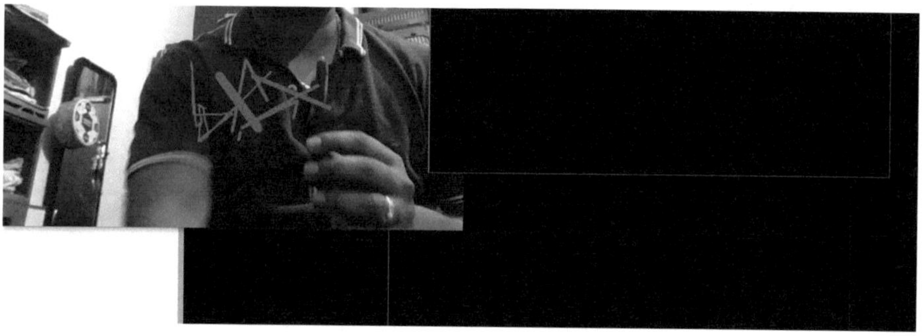

Detecting Lanes

We all know that self-driving cars are one of the biggest newsmakers in the automotive industry nowadays. Cars know when to turn left, when to stop, how to read traffic signs, and so on. In this section we learn how a car looks at a lane in a highway and understands its meaning, thus defining its boundaries—in other words, not leaving the lane. If you want to become an expert in programming self-driving cars, there is a nanodegree program by Udacity that you can attend.

To get started, we first need to calibrate our camera. Because the entire self-driving car concept depends on the accuracy of the camera, we *must* calibrate it. To do so, we use a function in OpenCV called `findChessboardCorners()`, which (as you might imagine) finds the internal corners of a given image of a chessboard.

```
def convert3D_to_2D(path, x, y):
rwp = np.zeros((y*x, 3), np.float32)
tmp = np.mgrid[0:x, 0:y].T.reshape(-1, 2)
rwp[:,:2] = tmp
rwpoints = []
```

```
imgpoints = []
images = glob.glob(path)
for fname in images:
    img = cv2.imread(fname)
    gray = cv2.cvtColor(img, cv2.COLOR_BGR2GRAY)
    corner_found, corners = cv2.findChessboardCorners(gray,
    (x,y), None)
    if corner_found == True:
        rwpoints.append(rwp)
        imgpoints.append(corners)
        cv2.drawChessboardCorners(img, (x,y), corners, corner_
        found)
return (rwpoints, imgpoints)
```

A complete line-by-line explanation of the code is provided in the Sharepoint. The previous code reads different chessboard images present in a directory, finds their internal corners, and saves the final points in two lists: `rwpoints` and `imgpoints`. `rwpoints` contain real space points in three dimensions; `imgpoints` points are in two dimensions. The function returns both lists.

Next, we use these two lists to calibrate the camera and then undistort the image. Undistortion means removing the noise and smoothing the image. In simpler terms, we say we convert the image from three dimensions to two dimensions. Let's look at the code:

```
def calibrate_camera(test_img_path, rwpoints, imgpoints):
    img = mpimg.imread(test_img_path)
    img_size = (img.shape[1], img.shape[0])
    ret, mtx, dist, rvecs, tvecs = cv2.
calibrateCamera(rwpoints, imgpoints, img_size, None, None)
    undst_img = cv2.undistort(img, mtx, dist, None, mtx)
    f, (ax1, ax2) = plt.subplots(1, 2, figsize=(20, 10))
```

```
    ax1.set_title("Original Image")
    ax1.imshow(img)
    ax2.set_title("Undistorted Image")
    ax2.imshow(undst_img)
    return (mtx, dist)
```

The `calibrateCamera()` function first tries to make the camera efficient by using the `rwpoints` and `imgpoints` lists. It gives us two important matrices—`mtx` and `dst`—to help us undistort the image. The output of the undistortion looks like this:

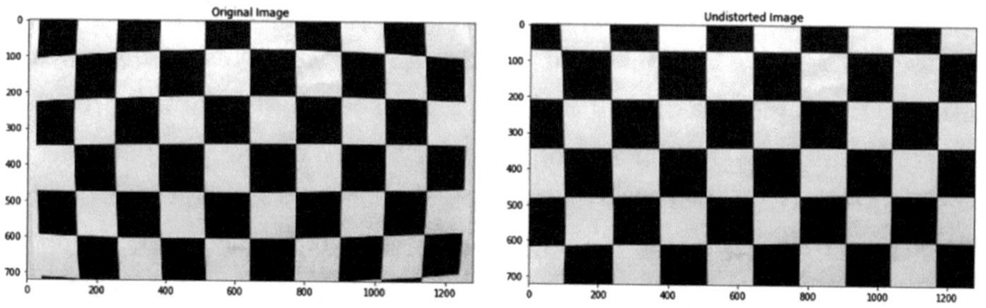

Because the undistortion is working fine, let's apply the same to a road image:

```
def undistort_test_img(mtx, dist):
    test_image = mpimg.imread("road.jpg")
    undistorted_img = cv2.undistort(test_image, mtx, dist,
    None, mtx)
    f, (ax1, ax2) = plt.subplots(1, 2, figsize=(20, 10))
    ax1.set_title("Original Image")
    ax1.imshow(test_image)
    ax2.set_title("Undistorted Image")
    ax2.imshow(undistorted_img)
```

After applying this above code to a test image, we get the following output:

Now that we have the image in two dimensions (an undistorted image), we need to perform perspective transformation. Perspective, in layman's terms, is the angle and direction at which you see a particular thing. So two people looking at a particular thing always have a different perspective.

In the case of self-driving cars, cameras always look at the road lines. These road lines are never constant, thus their perspective keeps changing. To make sure the perspective for the camera always remains constant, we use perspective transformation.

The first thing we need to do is select four points in the lane, which guide us during perspective transformation. We select these points randomly. I hard-coded these points, so that they match the exact positions in the image.

```
src = np.float32([
        [203, 720],
       [585, 460],
        [695, 460],
        [1127, 720]])
dst = np.float32([
        [270, 720],
       [310, 0],
        [960, 0],
        [1010, 720]])
```

Now we give these two points to the function `getPerspectiveTransform()` to find the perspective transformation matrix and the inverse perspective transformation matrix:

```
M = cv2.getPerspectiveTransform(src, dst)
Minv = cv2.getPerspectiveTransform(dst, src)
```

We use these matrices for perspective transformation, and then later to return to our original image. First, let's see how to do the transformation:

```
test_image = mpimg.imread("road.jpg")
img_size = (test_image.shape[1], test_image.shape[0])
undistorted_img = cv2.undistort(test_image, mtx, dist, None, mtx)
i = draw_polygon(undistorted_img)
warped = cv2.warpPerspective(undistorted_img, M, img_size)
f, (ax1, ax2) = plt.subplots(1, 2, figsize=(20, 10))
ax1.set_title("Original Image")
ax1.imshow(i)
ax2.set_title("Undistorted Warped Image")
ax2.imshow(warped)
```

When we run this code, we get the following output:

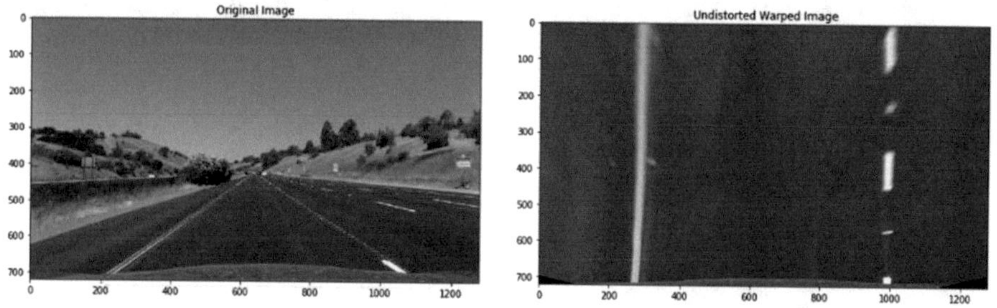

Finally we have the transformed image. We convert the image to binary format, so the camera is able to find and understand the road lines. To do this, we use Sobel transformation. This edge detection algorithm helps us track the lines present on the road.

So, as mentioned, we undistort and change the perspective of the image, then convert it to a binary image (a combination of black and white). After that, we apply further transformations.

```
img = cv2.undistort(test_image, mtx, dist, None, mtx)
color_binary, edges_img = find_edges(img)
img_size = (edges_img.shape[1], edges_img.shape[0])
warped_img = cv2.warpPerspective(edges_img, M, img_size,
flags=cv2.INTER_LINEAR)
```

To find the edges, we have created a function called `find_edges`, which is used to detect edges, and get color and binary images containing those edges. We then apply the `warpPerspective()` function to use matrix `M` for perspective transformation of the image generated.

When we apply the previous code to the original image, we get the following outputs:

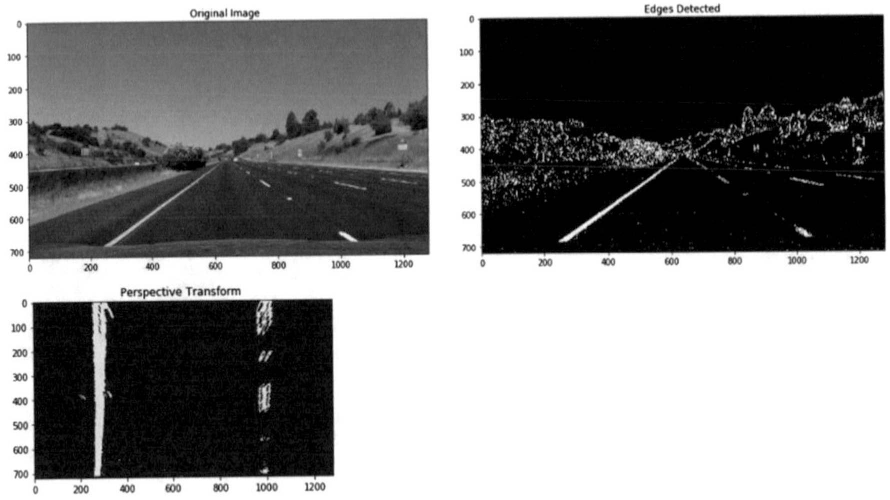

Last, we wrap back the images we created onto the original image. Only then will we be able to determine whether the camera is detecting the road lines correctly. To do this, we use the second matrix: `Minv`.

We again use the function `warpPerspective()`, but with `Minv` instead of `M`:

```
newwarp = cv2.warpPerspective(color_warp, Minv, (warped_img.
shape[1], warped_img.shape[0])
```

`color_warp` is used to create the image that contains the road lines the code detected, and fills them with color. We retain our original perspective by using `Minv`. A detailed explanation of the code is given in the Sharepoint. Let's look at the output:

So, we have successfully detected road lines. The car has detected the road and the path on which it has to travel.

APPENDIX

Important Concepts and Terminology

Adaboost

Adaboost is a technique that uses multiple classification algorithms throughout the training data. First we take a random sample from the dataset and call it a *training set*. Adaboost assigns weights to each and every example in the training set. After that, the first classifier is run. When the classification is done, Adaboost looks at the misclassified examples in the training set. They are then assigned greater weights, as are the correctly classified examples. This happens so that when the second classifier is run, it takes into consideration examples with greater weights.

In addition, weights are assigned to classifiers as well. When the classifier gives an output, its error is calculated. Based on the intensity of the error, weights are assigned. If the error is less than 50% accurate, the classifier is given a negative weight; otherwise, it's given a positive weight. Fifty percent accuracy equates to a weight of zero.

H. Singh, *Practical Machine Learning and Image Processing*,
https://doi.org/10.1007/978-1-4842-4149-3

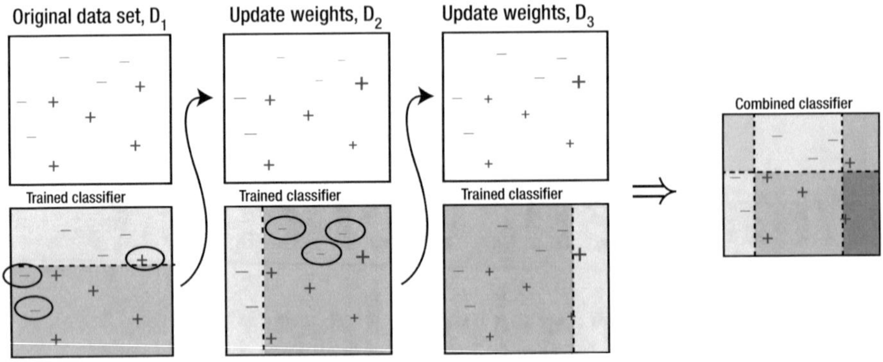

Figure A-1. *(Credit: Research Gate)*

Adaboost is used most widely in face recognition. We have already seen how we used Haar cascades, or LBPH cascades, for detecting the faces. Adaboost plays a very big role in that.

XGBoost

XGBoost stands for Extreme Gradient Boosting. It is one of the most highly used classification and regression algorithms. You will find that winners of mostly all the analytics competitions like kaggle, KDNuggets, Hackerearth, and so on, use this concept. XGBoost uses the gradient descent approach to find the best solution to a problem. Its computational power, as well as the precision of its results, make it so powerful. It uses multiple CPU cores to give faster computations.

Instead of assigning weights (as done with Adaboost), XGBoost looks at the mismatched errors (also called *residuals*) for each training example and tries to create a regression model over them. Thus, for each and every iteration, a new model is created, that is nothing but gradients. Its output minimizes error as much as possible.

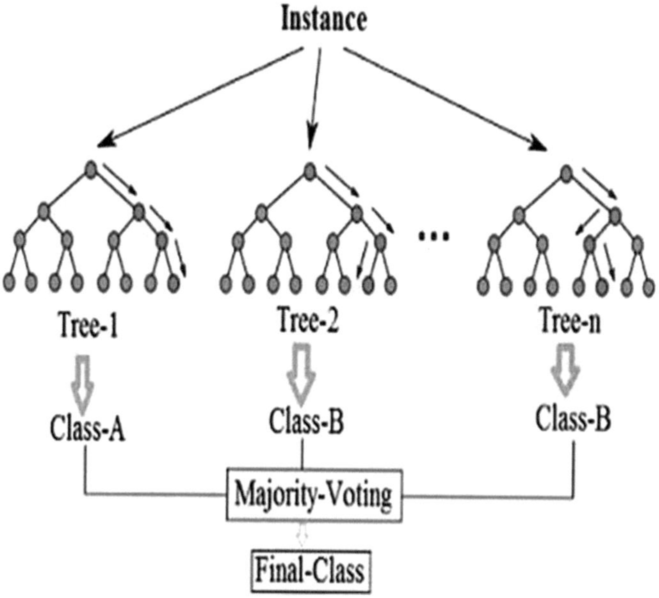

Figure A-2.

Pulse-coupled Neural Networks

Pulse-coupled neural networks (PCNNs) were conceptualized after the industry acquired an understanding of a cat's visual cortex, which is the area of a cat's brain that processes visual information. A PCNN can be used for segmenting an image, reducing noise, generating features, and more. When we apply PCNN to images, each and every neuron corresponds to one pixel in an image. Also, all the neurons are connected to each other to receive stimuli. Information given to each neuron, and the information passed by one neuron to another, is later combined using an activation function, which results in a pulse output. PCNNs are more effective than other image processing models because they are robust to noise, they take care of geometric variations present inside an image, and so on. To study an implementation of PCNNs in pattern recognition, see `https://www.raulmuresan.ro/Papers/PCNN.pdf`.

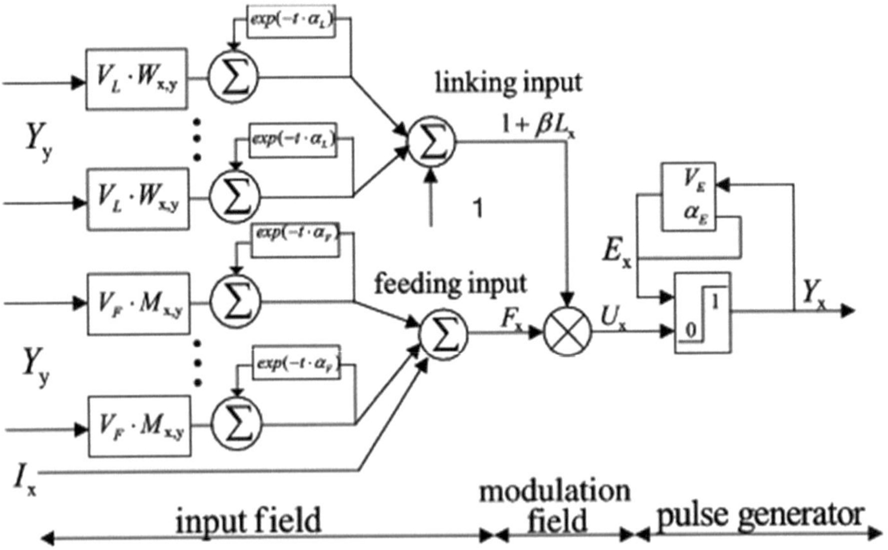

Figure A-3. *(Credit: Research Gate)*

Gradient Descent

Gradient descent is one of the best approaches used for optimization. When we talk about machine learning, there's always some errors in prediction. This error is denoted by the cost function. If the cost function's value is zero, our accuracy of prediction is 100%. To keep the value of the cast function low, we use a gradient descent approach.

For example, let's define the cost function as f(x) = ax + b. a and b are the parameters. Imagine that the curve of this function is similar to a bowl. First we give some random values to a and b, which puts our cost function at a particular position on a curve. Our aim is to change the values of a and b in such a way that the cost function reaches the bottom of the bowl/curve. To do this, we use a learning rate. At the end of gradient descent, we get values for a and b that are either zero or very, very close to it.

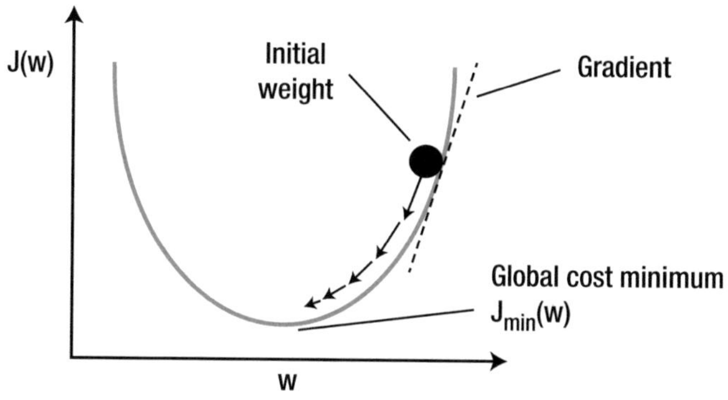

Figure A-4. *(Credit: Hackernoon)*

Stochastic Gradient Descent

Stochastic gradient descent is the faster version of the normal gradient descent algorithm. Using the normal gradient descent, a and b are updated for every record present in the dataset, which makes the process very time-consuming if the dataset is large. Stochastic gradient descent, on the other hand, updates the data after one complete training instance is completed, not in individual training records. This makes the process faster.

With this algorithm, you may find that the cost function jumps around on the curve, but it finally does reach the bottom of the curve.

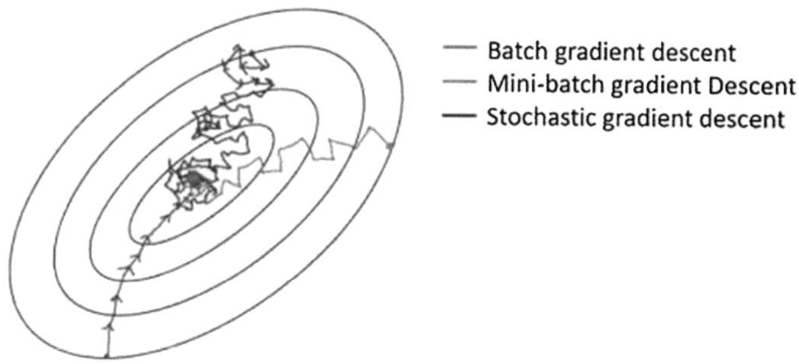

Figure A-5. *(Credit: Towards Data Science)*

AdaDelta

AdaDelta belongs to the family of stochastic gradient descent approaches. Using this method, apart from its stochastic gradient descent features, special importance is given to the value of coefficients. This is called *parameter tuning*. Aside from this, the learning rate is not initialized with any kind of default value; it is updated automatically. Therefore, it involves the least amount of manual intervention, and hence better accuracy.

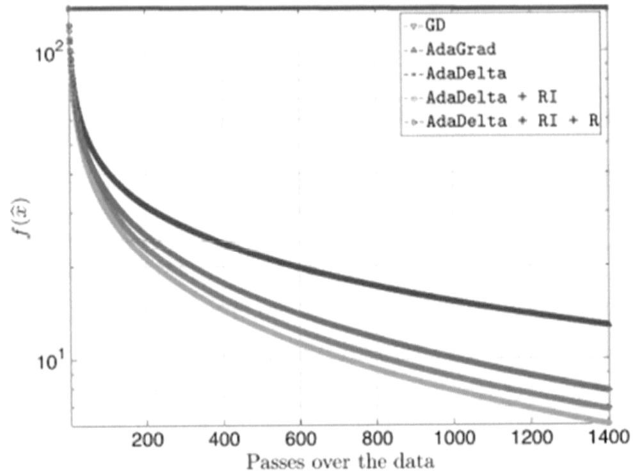

Figure A-6. *Comparative analysis of various optimization techniques (Credit: akyrillidis.github.io)*

Canny Edge Detector

As its name suggests, the Canny Edge Detector is used for finding the edges present inside an image. After finding the edges, we can use it for different purposes, such as image segmentation, feature extraction, detection, and so on. Using this algorithm, the first step is to remove the noise present in the image. If not removed, the wrong image may be detected and the analysis may be affected negatively.

After the image is smoothed, we apply Sobel transformation to it, to find the image gradients. This is a major step, because it helps us find the edges. We get the magnitude of the gradients as well as their direction. The next step is to remove all those parts of the image that are not required. This step finally gives us edges, but we aren't sure whether they are correct.

The final step determines whether the final image contains edges that are actually edges. To do this, threshold values are used. Any edge with a value greater than the threshold is considered an edge; otherwise, it's not.

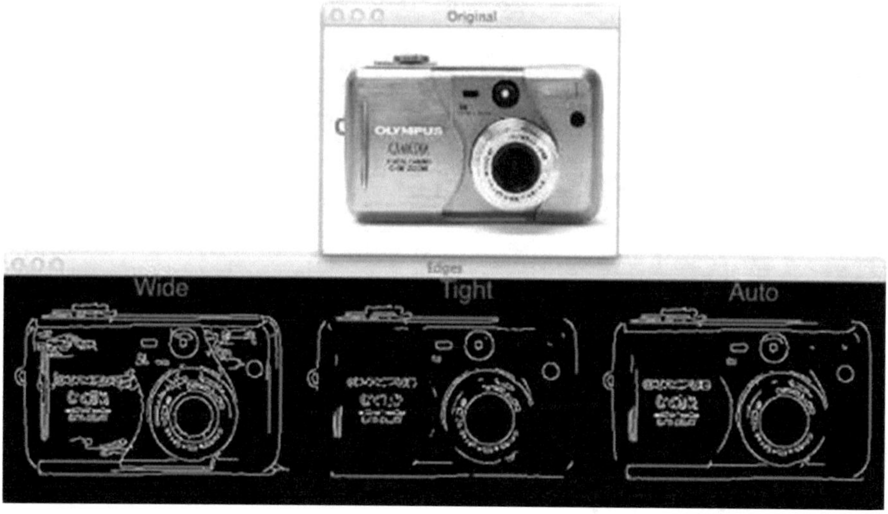

Figure A-7. *(Credit: pyimagesearch)*

Sobel Transformation

One of the main uses of Sobel transformation is to detect edges. A 3×3 matrix is used that traverses the pixels of an image horizontally and vertically. It is similar to kernels in CNSNs. The output of Sobel includes derivatives.

You may be wondering: Why do we use gradients? Suppose we have selected a portrait of a girl. If some of her hair is on her face, then the color tone changes suddenly from skin color to black. This must be represented as an edge—and for this we need gradients. The greater the value of gradients, the lesser the difference in tone. Therefore, to detect edges, we need to know all those pixel locations with a gradient value greater than a specific threshold.

Figure A-8. *(Credit: Research Gate)*

Haar Cascade

LBPH Face Recognition

Image Moments

Image moments are special weights assigned to specific pixels based on the properties we require. In general, we determine image moments after we have completed image segmentation.

Figure A-9. *(Credit: OpenCV)*

Image Contours

Suppose we have two points. If we draw a line—one that is not necessarily straight—to connect those two points, then that lime is considered a contour. Thus, contours are used to detect and analyze shapes, to perform different types of recognition, and so on.

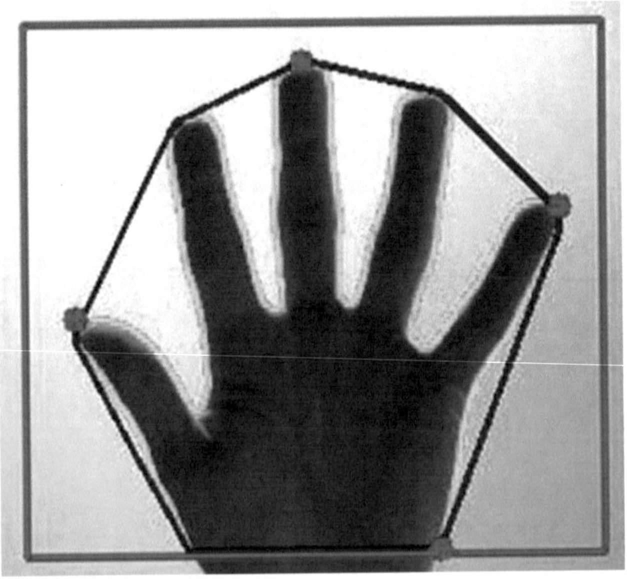

Figure A-10. *(Credit: Pyimagesearch)*

Chessboard Corners Function

When we take pictures using camera, the image may come distorted through dilation, erosion, and so on. Also, if we scale the image up or down, the scaling factor may not be same.

Therefore, to eliminate these issues, we must calibrate the camera. But first, we need to find a few points that tells us about accuracy. To find these points, we are given a chessboard image for reference. Our code finds the internal corners present in the board. If we use an 8 × 8 board, the code needs to find the 7 × 7 internal corners. When we get this right, we get a two-point array that we use to calibrate the camera.

Figure A-11. *(Credit: OpenCV)*

Calibrate Camera Function

When we have determined the internal chessboard corners, and got our point always, we give them to calibrate camera function. This function helps us take care of distortion, rotation, scaling, and so on. It also returns a camera matrix, distortion matrix, rotational matrix, and so on. We use them later in our code.

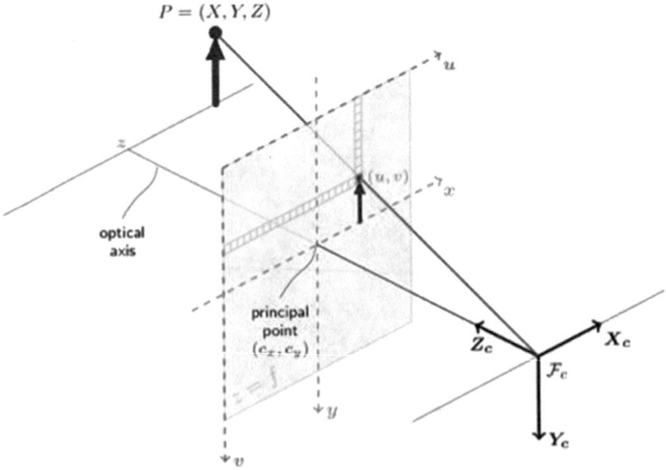

Figure A-12. *(Credit: OpenCV)*

Perspective Transformation Function

Suppose we have an image, but we want to see it from a different viewpoint. Let's say we select a satellite image of a location and want to overlay it with a drone image that is of exactly the same place, and scale, as the satellite image. To do this, we use perspective transformation.

The function we use is called `getPerspectiveTransform()`, and it is present in OpenCV. We give the image for which we want to change the perspective, and then we give the matrix used for the transformation. The final image we receive has a changed perspective.

To return this image to the original, we use the function `warpPerspective()`, which registers the image on the original image.

Figure A-13. *(Credit: Pyimagesearch)*

Index

H. Singh, *Practical Machine Learning and Image Processing*,
https://doi.org/10.1007/978-1-4842-4149-3

S

T

U

V, W

X

Y, Z

Printed in the United States
By Bookmasters